KU-098-087

COMPLETE GUIDE TO FUNDRAISING

P W and P F Sterrett

2000

Copyright © PW and PF Sterrett 1988, 2001

All rights reserved. No part of this publication may be reproduced, stored in a retrieval system, or transmitted in any form or by any means, electronic, mechanical, photocopying, recording, or otherwise without the prior permission of the publishers.

First published in 1998 by Mercury Books

This revised edition published in 2001 by Management Books 2000 Ltd
Cowcombe House
Cowcombe Hill
Chalford
Gloucestershire GL6 8HP
Tel. 01285 760 722
Fax. 01285 760 708
E-mail: m.b.2000@virgin.net

Printed and bound in Great Britain by Biddles, Guildford

This book is sold subject to the condition that it shall not, by way of trade or otherwise, be lent, resold, hired out, or otherwise circulated without the publisher's prior consent in any form of binding or cover other than that in which it is published and without a similar condition including this condition being imposed upon the subsequent purchaser.

British Library Cataloguing in Publication Data is available
ISBN 1-85252-369-7

FOREWORD

As a young man, I joined a group of volunteers who wanted to raise money to purchase a lift for a home for physically disabled people. We needed a lot of money, and I soon realised that we would never reach our target by raising it in the usual time-consuming ways. We were gaining very little profit in return for long hours of hard work.

I then began to think of novel fund-raising ideas that would attract public interest and support, and bring us in the money that we needed quickly. Happily my inventive ideas worked! More than that, they were so successful that within a very short time we were able to buy and install the lift, and a lot of other expensive equipment as well.

News of our success spread, and soon I was inundated with requests for fund-raising ideas, help and advice. People were so enthusiastic and so excited with the results of my efforts that it was evident my skills were benefiting many other fund-raising groups as well as my own.

It is not lack of enthusiasm or motivation to succeed that causes the downfall of would-be fund-raisers. It is the inability to think of new games and competitions that will raise money for charity and the failure to think projects through in a professional and businesslike way. Poor communications between members of the team can also produce complications which could be avoided. Most people have very little experience in fund-raising, and for a beginner there is a lot to learn. I hope this book will answer many questions on fund-raising and give inexperienced people a chance to make money for their cause.

It was people's thirst for knowledge and their enthusiasm to learn that prompted me to write my first book on fund-raising, Fund-Raising for Charity, Cash for Good Causes. This book was a big success because it was the first of its kind to present fund-raising games and competitions. When it was launched in 1979, my mail was full of letters requesting help to raise money for worthwhile causes, and I extended my fund-raising hobby to giving seminars and lectures to groups who want to develop their fund-raising talents.

After these teaching sessions, I am often thanked for my help in giving new fund-raising ideas and renewing confidence in fund-raising. People say they will forget disasters of the past and look forward to making a lot more money for their causes. I am always glad to stimulate enthusiasm to succeed, but I always give one warning: 'Never forget your fund-raising problems because you must remember not to make the same mistakes again. Learn from problems and benefit from them in future years.'

I am often fortunate to share the pleasures of people who have developed a new attitude and technique to fund-raising. They are thrilled with the results of their efforts, and they are proud to tell me how successfully they have used my fund-raising ideas and advice to make huge profits for their cause. It is heart-warming to hear of great achievements after so many heart-aches of the past for many such groups.

People should be proud of their fund-raising efforts, and yet often the opposite is true. Time and time again I am told of horrifying fund-raising disasters, caused by innocent mismanagement that could have been avoided with just a little knowledge and expertise by the groups concerned. By repeating some of the stories in this book, I hope that others can learn to avoid making the same mistakes.

Patricia, my wife, has been happy to share my fund-raising experiences, and it is with her encouragement and assistance that this book has been produced. We hope that my ideas will eliminate the hazards and pitfalls of fund-raising and make the occupation both profitable and enjoyable for readers. If the book succeeds in our aim to guide and direct people in the art of making funds without tears, then our efforts will have been well rewarded!

Paddy Sterrett

Contents

Part 1

PLANNING FOR
FUND-RAISING

1

QUESTION YOUR FUND-RAISING POTENTIAL

It is sometimes hard to be honest with yourself, but if you really have any feelings for the hopes and prosperity of the group in which you are involved, you should answer the questions below honestly. Decide for yourself whether you are a real asset to the group or whether you are only a badge-wearer who enjoys the status of membership because it gives a degree of self-esteem to be seen to belong to a worthwhile organisation.

Answer the questions truthfully, and if you find that most of the answers are 'don't know' or 'no' then have the courage and good sense to retire. If you are doing nothing to promote the cause you should direct your talents into something that you can enjoy doing, and make room for someone who will offer more positive aid.

- Why did you become involved in fund-raising? Was it to help the group?

- Do you really enjoy fund-raising activity?

- Do you honestly believe that you contribute to your group's fund-raising activities to the best of your ability?

- Would you like to be of more help to your group?

- Do you get along well with most of the members of your group?

- Do you feel a sense of inner satisfaction after a successful fund-raising project, or do you think: 'Thank God that's over!'

- Do you employ the same amount of thought and detail to your fund-raising schemes as you do to your business or profession?

- Does the prospect of helping in an exciting project give you pleasure?

- Do you try to use your imagination to think up new competitions which will raise money for your cause? (Daily events can be used to advantage: *for example, guess the miles travelled to and from work in a week by the average sales [person.* In this competition you would ask friends who are sales reps to record their mileage for you, and take the average mileage from about twelve results.)

- Do the needs of your fund-raising group occupy a strong place in your thoughts?

If the answer to most of these questions is 'yes' you are a good fund-raiser!

2

WHAT ARE THE QUALITIES OF A GOOD FUND-RAISER?

Fund-raising is an occupation pursued by many people every year. Some find it a challenging hobby and derive a great deal of pleasure from it, whilst the majority find it hard work and tedious. They do it because they want to help their group to achieve a goal, or because they want to help someone less fortunate than themselves, or because their efforts will help a relative or friend. All these motives are commendable, and volunteers should be given credit for working hard at their task. Certainly they will do all that is possible to achieve the aims of the group.

Sadly, good intentions and worthwhile motives do not automatically ensure success. Many volunteers will end up with disasters and disappointments because of their inexperience and because they do not put sufficient time and effort into the planning and administration of their events. Some find that they are unprepared for the hard work that is needed to make the venture a success. Others are unwilling to give the time and so take short cuts which inevitably lead to failure.

Many volunteers are a handicap rather than a help to their cause. Only those who are not afraid of hard work and who are able and willing to give the necessary time to fulfil their task, will finally achieve their charity's goals.

☑ Fund-raisers must enjoy the work.

☑ They must accept the challenge cheerfully.

15

☑ They must derive a great deal of satisfaction from the work.

☑ They must be able to work enthusiastically with a team of volunteers.

☑ They must be able to accept guidance from a leader.

☑ They must have the time, the patience and the skill to make their ventures a real success.

3

FIND A GOOD LEADER

A good leader is essential to your fund-raising committee, and must have some special qualities if the group is to benefit fully from his or her presence:

- ☑ The leader must be an efficient and capable organiser.

- ☑ Leaders must be able to plan an event in every detail.

- ☑ Leaders must be able to communicate with their helpers. They should enjoy working with people and should be able to lead without causing offence.

- ☑ A leader must be able to motivate others, and inspire them with enthusiasm and zeal.

- ☑ Leaders must be good judges of people. They must get to know the committee and helpers well, and be able to recognise and use the talents and abilities of individual members of the group. They must also be able to understand each person's strengths and weaknesses in order to direct and guide them in a way that they can accept and enjoy.

Leaders with these qualities must benefit their cause at the end of the day, so it is important to choose a leader who has these qualities, rather than choose the first person who agrees to accept the role just to fill a vacancy.

Fund-raising is not an easy task, and it does take a very special type of person to be really successful. People who accept the work as a chore can often be more of a hindrance than a help because they are impatient to finish the task and their lack of interest can rub off onto the very people from whom they are seeking support. If people are shy, reticent, embarrassed or unconvinced about the work they are doing, they cannot possibly inspire confidence in their group or in the public. If they take chances to finish a project quickly, or make rash decisions, they can lead the group into chaos and financial ruin.

Most people can learn to take a positive attitude to fund-raising, and as they gain confidence they begin to enjoy the role. First they must *believe* in what they are trying to do. They must be clear about the aims and objectives of their fund-raising group and they must approve of the fund-raising scheme in operation. Then, if they are sure about the role they have to play, they will rise to the challenge and feel happy about what they are doing.

Fund-raising experiences for many are limited to helping to sell raffle tickets, shaking collection tins, or helping at jumble sales and coffee mornings. It is hard to get excited about any of these activities. Any form of begging for money without giving something in return can be resented by the public; and fund-raisers find that a negative response to their endeavours can be quite soul-destroying.

After reading this book, you will be able to devise new fund-raising ideas that offer excitement and a challenge to the public. Helpers can actually enjoy giving people a chance to enter an interesting competition if they provide contestants with something in return for their money, such as a little fun, excitement and intrigue, plus a challenge to their ability and skills, and the offer of a worthwhile prize for the winner!

The fund-raising ideas in this book appeal to people because they are out of the ordinary. They have all proved popular money spinners for fund-raising groups, and they can raise quite a lot of money for your cause without the need of expensive equipment.

Remember, if you apply your efforts to fund-raising with the same criteria you apply to business life, you cannot go far wrong:

1. Give value for money
2. Plan well in advance
3. Master the techniques

Don't forget to look carefully at your attitudes and motives, as once you start thinking positively about fund-raising, you will find the experience both emotionally rewarding and financially beneficial.

4

HOW TO MAKE YOUR FUND-RAISING VENTURES SUCCESSFUL

Local authorities cannot offer the same financial support to voluntary groups that they used to and big firms no longer enjoy tax benefits from donating to charity. Many companies' profits have fallen and people are more discerning about how they spend their money, with the result that many voluntary organisations are struggling for survival. There are many thousands of charities and other voluntary groups attempting to raise money to develop, maintain or improve vital services for the community. These groups are all competing with one another for our money, and pressures are greater than ever before. Hazards and pitfalls await the organisers around every corner.

To be forewarned is to be forearmed, and when people are aware of the pitfalls, they can approach their fund-raising schemes with confidence of success. Consider the following tips, and your group will avoid many problems.

1.   *Do not try to run an event without a competent leader*

The leader is the most important member of the group. He or she knows the abilities of each member. The leader must direct the entire event with confidence and authority and be aware of what is happening at every stage of a project. Do not choose a leader just because he or she is popular and well liked; choose someone who is an efficient organiser, who has a flair for motivating people, and who has the will to succeed. Leaders who can plan, organise and run an event, and at the same time stimulate their committee members and helpers, are worth their weight in gold. If the leader does not have these qualities, then your project is in trouble from the start.

2. Do not try to run an event without a committee

Elect a special fund-raising committee from the onset and decide that this committee has the final say in its own administrations. Disruptive members of the main group can project despondency and gloom to fund-raising members, and this will quell initiative and enthusiasm. If there is a proper fund- raising committee, it won't be side-tracked by ill-informed people who offer destructive criticism.

3. Helpers must be given support from the onset

The leader will assess cach helper's ability and must delegate tasks accordingly. Helpers must have a clear understanding of the role they have to play, and they also need to know the role of each other helper in the group. Helpers who are not happy with the jobs they have been asked to do should be directed to something more suitable to their skills. It is important that helpers know to whom they should turn if they need advice and guidance, or chaos can result.

Whilst the project is running, helpers should wear some form of identification as this saves a lot of confusion on the day.

4. Check that your event does not clash with a similar event being held at the same time by another voluntary group

Fund-raising events often clash at Christmas, Easter or during the summer holidays, and a really good event is often spoiled by coinciding dates. Sometimes two or more organisations find they are holding similar events on the same day. This is detrimental to all the groups concerned, and it can be avoided. To do so, arrange an annual meeting of a voluntary liaison group. Invite a member from each fund-raising group in your area to attend, and agree on the dates that each organisation will hold its various events. A meeting like this can help to avoid duplication of similar events, as well as clashing of dates, and it will reduce tension and misunderstandings between groups.

5.   Plan the details of your event carefully

Having decided how much money you need to raise for your cause, you must then make decisions on the following points:

- What fund-raising project will help you to raise the money?
- How many people will you need to cater for?
- How many helpers will you need?
- What equipment will you need?
- How are you going to advertise your event?
- What tickets and printed matter will you need?
- What venue will you choose to hold the event?
- Where are you going to find your prizes?
- How can the group avoid spending money?
- What additional methods of raising money can be held at the same time?

6.   Be careful not to break the law when running an event

By contravening the Gaming and Lotteries Acts, your group can plunge into great financial hardship without even realising they are breaking the law. It is important to be aware of how you stand legally when running a charitable event, and it is wise to purchase copies of the appropriate Acts from the Stationery Office. Fund-raising groups would be well advised to obtain the most up-to-date information on the law on lotteries and gaming. Sources include the National Council for Voluntary Organisations – visit their website at **www.ncvo-vol.uk** – or the Directory for Social Change at **www.dsc.org.uk**. Booklets are available that help to explain the Gaming and Lotteries Acts in terms understandable to the layman who is trying to raise funds for charity without getting into trouble with the law.

Some of the laws in relation to fund-raising are difficult to comprehend – even for those involved in trying to maintain the laws! If there is any doubt about the legality of a venture, ask the advice of the Gaming and Lotteries Board or a legal adviser who has knowledge of the legislation. The police can advise on many of the relevant laws, like those concerning the sale of alcoholic drink on unlicensed premises, but the gaming and lottery laws are wide and complicated and so easy to break! Even the police have been known to employ a QC to decide whether a fund-raising project is legal under the Gaming and Lotteries Acts. It is essential to make sure that your choice of event will not create trouble with the law because otherwise you risk losing any profit that your group may have earned.

7. Make sure that your games and competitions are organised fairly

It is important to be able to prove to the public that your fund-raising projects are fair and above suspicion. You must take the following precautions to avoid criticism:

1. Write down the name and address of the winner.

2. Advertise the winning numbers as well as the name and address of the winner.

3. Make sure that the date, time and place of a raffle draw are made public. Advertise these details properly.

4. Publish the details of your income and expenses.

5. Publish details of any profits and losses, and give details on how profits are to be spent.

6. Keep good records of everything you do.

8.   Make sure that you choose a suitable venue

It is important to choose a venue which is suitable for your fund-raising operation. You need sufficient space for stalls, if you are running a fete, as well as plenty of space for people to move about without overcrowding and congestion. Choose a site which is big enough for your expected turnout and accessible from the main roads. Make sure that there is ample car parking space, and if necessary use helpers to direct the cars to make the best use of the parking space available.

Check that the gates to a field are wide enough to take large vehicles if these are to be used to transport equipment.

Remember that a small event can be lost in too large an acreage of ground, and the atmosphere can be destroyed.

9.   Beware of traffic problems

If you expect a large number of cars, then it is courteous and helpful to notify the police. Their help and advice is invaluable. They will direct the traffic, help to avoid traffic hold-ups caused by cars arriving and leaving the site, and prevent accidents. Traffic guidance from the police will obviously benefit all concerned.

10.   Make sure that your event is insured

When holding an indoor event, make sure that the owner of the building has the premises fully insured for public liability and fire.

If you plan to organise games which involve moving equipment, it is wise to insure against injury to members of the public, even if there is only a remote chance of danger to people. Every eventuality should be fully insured.

11.   Avoid over-spending

It is foolish to spend money on an event unless you know for certain that it can be recouped in some way. Paying exorbitant fees to professional artists, hiring tents and marquees, or spending vast sums of money on printing, prizes and administration can cripple a group's fund-raising endeavours.

Remember, if you pay £1,000 for someone to open a fete, then you are going to need 10,000 tenpence pieces in income before you can begin to make any profit for your cause.

- Decide how much money is needed to start your project, and plan how this money is to be obtained.

- Find sources which will offer you the loan of equipment.

- Ask local business people for a donation towards the event, perhaps in return for some publicity.

- Ask retail shops to donate prizes.

- Think what will be a realistic entrance fee to charge in order to attract the largest number of people.

- Decide which are the most exciting games and competitions that you can organise – which games will encourage people to part with their money and play willingly and cheerfully. If people like the idea of the challenge you offer, then you have chosen a winner!

You can save money by sharing equipment with other fund-raising groups in your area. Advertise what equipment you have for hire and which items you need to borrow at your voluntary liaison committee. At this meeting you may agree to share the cost of an expensive item of equipment that you can all use.

Some groups make extra money by charging a small fee for the hire of expensive equipment that they have purchased. Such fees help to reimburse the cost.

12. *Choose imaginative attractions that will appeal to the public*

A big failing on behalf of many fund-raising groups is that they believe they do not need to make much effort to give people something in return for their money. If they represent a worthy cause, they think people should part with their money willingly. This is an unfortunate attitude because people look for value for money and will not contribute generously to a cause that gives them nothing in return – even if it is a very worthwhile charity.

Choose one of the fund-raising ideas in this book, or use your imagination to think of inspirational new ideas that will fascinate people. The public will appreciate your efforts, and will support your event in favour of another group that hasn't taken so much trouble. Beware of using the same uninspired event each year. Repetition is monotonous and does not encourage people to participate. Always think of new ways to uplift and improve an annual event.

To me, flag days are a boring and uninspired way to raise money. Many people don't approve of this form of begging and will do anything to avoid the collection box! Also, most helpers are embarrassed by having to attract attention. They have nothing to give people for their money except one of those self-adhesive flags, and many people who do part with a few coins will refuse to take the offering.

I know of one occasion when 209 flag sellers trampled the streets of a big city from 9.30 am until 3.00 pm. It had been a long day and the sellers were cold and disillusioned by public apathy. Afterwards, they were shattered to learn that among them they had collected only £478.42. If they had all dipped into their own pockets and contributed three pounds each into the kitty, they would have been saved a miserable day and the indignity of public scorn. Better still, their charity would have raised over £100 more money! Each of the helpers vowed never to shake a tin in front of people again.

Everyone likes to participate in fun activities which are mentally or physically challenging. When people are encouraged to test their skills in anticipation of a worthwhile prize, they will be willing to pay a lot of money to try to master a game, especially if they find it exciting and fun to play. Most people enjoy some form of a gamble, and if you cater for this instinct you will be rewarded with satisfied customers. It sometimes pays to do a little research on the likes and dislikes of a neighbourhood. When you provide the right sort of stimulation, you will get all the public support that you need.

13. Don't be afraid to use advertising to supplement your income

Many charities lose a very lucrative additional income because their members have never considered advertising. You do not have to be an expert in promotion to succeed; just try the following advertising outlets and you will be surprised at the additional monies you can receive:

1. Many firms are looking for new outlets to advertise their products. Find the names of those who are advertising in local newspapers and ask them to provide you with prizes in return for allowing them to advertise their product or service at your fund-raising event.

2. If you are using a refreshment tent at your fete, find four firms who will be willing to advertise their product on posters which can be attached to the four sides of the tent. Advertisements for tea, coffee, soft drinks or foodstuffs will draw attention to the tent and the fees you get paid for displaying them will more than meet the cost of hiring the tent.

3. Ask tea and coffee firms for free supplies of their product in return for advertising the fact that their product is being sold.

4. Make sure that you sell all your advertising space in advance of the event. This money can be used for the hire of equipment that you have not been able to borrow free of charge.

14. Avoid poor attendances to your event

Inclement and unpredictable weather conditions have marred the success of many an excellent fund-raising project. Poor attendances greatly reduce an expected profit, but the problem can be overcome in the following ways:

1. Insure against bad weather with an insurance company that offers compensation for losses incurred in this way.

2. Organise an exciting competition which will ensure that

people attend your event, whatever the weather. If they have been involved in a game during a period leading up to your event, and hope to secure a prize, they will attend on the day to find out if they have won.

3. Sell tickets for your event in advance. If people have purchased their entry ticket, they will not like it to be wasted.

4. Offer a free competition entry like the Advertising Competition below. This will bring in a good revenue from advertisers and at the same time it will be fun for contestants to play. It will encourage greater attendance when it is advertised as a free chance to win a prize.

The Advertising Game

First find 20 firms who will each pay £50 to advertise at your event. For this fee you can promise your sponsors that every person who buys a ticket will not only read the advertisements on the day, but they will write them down and take them home for the whole family to read. You can guarantee this by supplying a free competition entry form on which all the advertisements on display at your event will be printed, and by offering a worthwhile prize. Everyone takes an interest.

On one side of the form, print a rectangle of squares in which the names of 20 products are hidden amongst randomly printed letters (see Figure 1). Contestants must find all the advertisements on display at the event, write down the correct wording of each, and ring all the advertisements in the rectangle of letters on the entry form. The forms are then returned to the secretary of the group (his or her name is printed on the form).

On an agreed date, all the winning entries will be put into a drum and the winning ticket will be drawn in a public place.

A suitable prize would be a small portable television set or a weekend holiday for two. You should be able to persuade a sponsor to donate the prize.

The Advertising Game is a popular means of advertising for manufacturers and retail outlets. If you obtain £50 for each advertisement your event will show a profit of £1,000 before you begin.

There will be a number of advertisements on display around the grounds of the Friendly Carnival, Spring Lane, Cornwall, on July 4. Read each of them and write down the wording in the space provided on the back of this form.

When you have done this, take the entry form home and try to locate the names of the advertisers in the rectangle of letters below. They may run back to front, up, down or diagonally. When you find the name, circle it with a pen.

When you have completed your entry, place it in the box provided at Anderson's Supermarket or post it to .... to arrive not later than June 1.

The decision of the judges is final and binding on all contestants.

Advertisers

AMURS OILS	B A D C A R F E R R Y S E R V I C E S K J E N E
BELLS CAR HIRE	Y T S A N F E U I E S A N K L D T N B P O C O N
SALE BUILDING SOCIETY	T A R N O L D S T V R E N T A L C F X I H N A C
SCHOOL ALES	E E T N N A O E F V G E W I O N H G A E N A E O
SUN ICES	I A E O H N T E R S Y G O N A I D H S R S R Y U
STAR CAR REPAIR	C O T N A S H R F U R N H A M F U R N I T U R E
DUNCAN CRISPS	O E A D T E E A O I A M L W U C N A I L O S B A
SPAR GARAGES	S C H O O L A L E S T E Y U R L C A S E N N R L
TELSTAR AUTOS	G L E U R C A S I N I C E S S R A I P E S I A E
DENBOW CYCLES	N A O B U Y B G E R T X A L O T N W A Y H N D H
MIRROR FILMS	I H L L T C A X A R C D E P I S S O R K O O F E
CAR FERRY SERVICES	D A L E S W H I S K Y I E A L U C A G F L H O C
ACRO PETROLEUM	L N T G A O P W R S A T S Y S D R T A A I T R B
DALES WHISKY	I I S L E B I A R A R O S A O C I V R O D A D I
CARTERS TYRES	U T T A A N W R T O O A Y R A S S L A F A R C T
ARNOLD TV RENTAL	B O T Z E E D R L L W C H O E D P E G I Y A R A
BRADFORD CREDIT BANK	E E R I S D R E S O T U A R A T S L E T S M E E
MARATHON INSURANCE	L L C N S A U E W R I F A O L A R L S A A I D D
JOHNSTONS HOLIDAYS	A R A G U M I R R O R F I L M S C A G S A W I I
FURNHAM FURNITURE	S S R O S F X B H U I R R E E O V C C S O T T T
CROSS TRAVEL SERVICES	B U R C O S G L A S S F I B R E K I T S C A B B
PROVIDENT SAVINGS BANK	B N E E A H J K L F E E E U I A S A S T H O A C
CANNONS DOUBLE GLAZING	A A P E E B E L L S C A R H I R E E D I O N N A
BURCOS GLASS FIBRE KITS	W O A P R O V I D E N T S A V I N G S B A N K P
	S S I U Y T R E S A B N O I U S S A R R A A S S
	D C R O S S T R A V E L S E R V I C E S A E R E

Name ....

Address .... Telephone ....

Only official entry forms accepted. No photocopies allowed.

Figure 1 – Sample entry form for the advertising competition

15. Provide adequate promotion and advertising of your event

It is important to advertise your event fully, and to make it sound attractive to the public so that people will know they will be missing an exciting day out if they do not attend.

Badly designed and amateurish looking posters do not attract the crowds. Remember that people are very much aware these days of the brilliance, colour and professionalism of most commercial advertising, on hoardings, in magazines, on television, in cinemas. You have to compete with that and still attract people to your event. Even attractive posters and notices, if placed in unsuitable places, will not draw in the people.

Promote your venture effectively and boldly, well in advance, over a wide area to ensure that everyone knows about the event and has an opportunity to come.

☑ Use colourful and professional-looking posters which are placed clearly so that the public can see them.

☑ Advertise in shop windows, libraries and in other public places.

☑ Send personal invitations to clubs and groups of people from organisations and societies that may have a special interest in your cause.

☑ Start to advertise the event as soon as the date, time and venue are known. Promote the event well in advance and remind people again near to the date.

☑ Hand out leaflets giving details of the event.

☑ Advertise the event on local radio and television as well as in your local newspapers.

☑ Start a competition or a raffle well in advance of a function, with the winning results to be made known at the event. This will publicise your activities and will ensure that people attend your function to see if they have won a prize.

16. Do not be afraid to use additional and unusual promotional ideas to benefit your group

There are untapped resources that can increase your income considerably. Why not try one of the following suggestions?

☑ Invite a mobile exhibition unit to promote a product at your event. There are several organisations that will pay a fee in return for a site for their vehicle. This provides easy money for your group because an exhibition unit is self-sufficient.

☑ Alternatively, invite a test-marketing firm to take a site at your event. This provides an opportunity for researchers to ask members of the public to sample a product and give an opinion. It is beneficial to these firms to operate in a venue where there are a large number of people. They may ask for the use of a caravan or other suitable unit but they will pay well for this service and for the use of your venue in which to operate.

☑ Contact representatives of local firms that are currently advertising in magazines and newspapers. Similarly contact the local area representatives of national firms who are advertising in this way. These people know whom to approach to make a quick deal on your behalf. Firms that are advertising in the media are usually in the market for new advertising outlets and may well be attracted to advertising at your event. Local representatives will give you support because they are likely to benefit from additional customers attracted by the promotion. You will find useful addresses of manufacturers in the Kelly's Directory at your local library.

17. Never tackle a project that is too big for the group

A fund-raising event that needs a great deal of planning and hard work can be doomed to failure if the committee are not willing to give it the time required. All helpers should be quite clear about the jobs they have been designated. If they are confident in what they are doing, it is half the battle. Lack of communication, fear of doing something wrong, and fear of upsetting other members of the group all lead to inefficiency and lack of action. Make sure that even the smallest detail has not been forgotten in administration. Small but important tasks, like remembering to welcome a speaker and make him or her feel comfortable and at ease until needed, can make all the difference to the efficient running of the event.

Helpers should all know to whom they must report if they need help. Don't wait until there is a crisis before letting people know where they can get the assistance that they need.

If you think you have enough confidence to organise a big event, make sure that there are sufficient reliable helpers willing to undertake all the various tasks to be done. Plan every stage of your event wisely, and in advance, and use your helpers effectively to ensure that all the tasks are performed efficiently and at the right time.

18. Make sure the prize is ready for the winner to collect

When you are promised a gift from a sponsor that is to be used as a prize, be sure to collect the item at the time it is offered. Always obtain some written evidence that the gift has been promised and that it will be available for collection on a specified day. It is very embarrassing when sponsors fail to keep their promise to provide a gift, and yet this often happens for a variety of reasons. If a prize of a Philips portable colour television is specified on an entry form, then this is the prize that must be offered as soon as the winner is known. The prize must be as advertised.

On one occasion, a sponsor had promised a substantial prize, possibly because he had hoped to benefit financially from his liaison with the charity, but an unexpected event put both the charity and its sponsor into difficulty: the firm was put into the hands of a receiver and it was unable to honour its promise. The charity could not find another sponsor and it had to meet the cost of the prize from its own reserves, and from the pockets of its members. In today's uncertain climate, a situation like this can easily happen, so take precautions!

19. Study new fund-raising ideas

If your group raises funds regularly, it is liable to be tempted to offer the same fund-raising ventures over and over again. It is important to provide a variety of games, events and competitions because your helpers as well as your public will become bored with too much repetition. Think of exciting new ideas that will provide a challenge and test people's initiative and skill. Make games fun to play and you will resolve problems of lethargy and indifference that can cause the death knell of any fund-raising group.

This book offers a selection of fund-raising ideas that have proved popular because they illustrate unusual and out-of- the-ordinary fund-raising games which capture the imagination. The first book on the subject of fund-raising proved very popular, and the new ideas in this book will also pave the way to successful and more exciting fund-raising ventures in future.

20. Think of new places to hold your fund-raising schemes

People like competitions that take them around shops, pubs and other public places. They also enjoy a game that stimulates their imagination and skill if they are sitting quietly in a club or pub for the evening. Test their powers of observation, or test their mental ability, and they will enjoy the challenge.

If you are fortunate enough to have a large number of petrol filling stations in your area, then run competitions on forecourts – with the consent of their proprietors of course!

Hospital leagues of friends can take advantage of the many facilities available in the hospitals they support. Patients have a lot of time to spare and will welcome an opportunity to be entertained. If you can give them something to occupy their time, it takes their minds off their hospital treatment. Invite patients to sell tickets for competitions and lotteries to friends and relatives who visit. Some lively fund-raising games can be played from a hospital bed.

A member of the league of friends can sit at the entrance to the hospital and invite visitors and hospital staff to participate in a large variety of fund-raising games and competitions which give a great deal of fun to the participants, and at the same time boost the funds for much needed equipment.

21. Think of extra ideas which will provide a bonus income on the day of your event

You must make use of every opportunity to raise extra cash whilst organising a fund-raising event. As well as your main event, devise several extra games and competitions which will persuade people to spend a little more money.

If you run a model racing car competition, people will pay for the opportunity to take part because they enjoy this activity and you are providing them with a new experience. At the same time you can raise extra money by asking the public to take bets on which car they think will win each race.

A novel way to persuade people to spend money at your stalls at a fete is to run a 'prize bell ring'. For this attraction you need to conceal an alarm bell in one of the stalls. People are told that there is a hidden timer and if the bell rings while someone is purchasing goods or paying a fee there they win an extra prize. The thought of winning something for nothing will draw more people to the stalls in the hope of being lucky. When the bell has rung, the timer must go back to the secretary's tent to be re-set. It is then hidden carefully in a different place.

Use some of the games listed in this book, and think of new ideas that will bring in that little extra cash for your cause on the day.

22. Confirm your bookings

Double booking of halls and sites for events is an all too common occurrence. It can result in your group losing money and wasting a lot of time and effort.

Make sure that your booking is officially recorded, and keep a copy of the booking on your file. Telephone confirmations must be followed by a letter or the booking may go to someone else and you may not know about the mistake until too late.

It is most frustrating to have to cancel an event because no suitable accommodation can be found in the time available, but if your booking has been confirmed in writing it is not your mistake, and you can claim compensation from the owners of the property or land for your loss of expected profits.

23. Do not get defeated by your attempts to find sponsors

When seeking a sponsorship, it is easy to become discouraged by rejections from people you thought would have taken more of an interest in your cause. If your first approach fails to get a positive result, then try again, and keep on trying until you find a sponsor. Others may already have succeeded in using the sponsors you were approaching. Some firms get inundated with calls for help, but with persistence you will eventually succeed in finding willing sponsorship.

24. Make sure that your venue is a suitable size

When running a fete, stalls should not be so congested that there is not sufficient space to move comfortably. Nor should there be too few stalls in a massive big area, because this can destroy the party atmosphere. Work out how many stalls you will need to make the venture a success, and how much space you will need to operate your venture in comfort.

25. Ensure that car parking facilities are available

Make sure that the field that you want to use as a car park is suitable for your needs. Will it be sufficiently dry in the event of heavy rain? You do not want cars to be bogged down in mud, nor do you want to use tractors to tow them out.

If there is any possibility of problems such as this, then try to find ground that has a firm base. If this is not possible, then borrow a large tractor that can be used for towing cars if necessary. At one fund-raising event in the south of England, an unscrupulous farmer took advantage of a situation such as this and he charged £3 a time for each vehicle that he rescued from the mud. That fund-raising group used the same field the following year, hoping that conditions would not be the same, but although the weather was good, sadly the group lost all its usual support because motorists remembered their plight of the previous year, and refused to attend.

26. Insure motor vehicles to carry the passengers and equipment you need

If you are planning to use a vehicle for any of your competitions, make sure that it is fully insured to cover the event and that is can be used for the purpose required (note that this applies equally to petrol, diesel, steam and even horse-drawn vehicles).

There have been occasions when mini-buses have been used with insurance cover that did not extend to the operation. One instance came to light when an accident occurred and a passenger was injured. It was discovered, too late, that passenger liability of the vehicle was restricted to employees of the firm that owned the bus, and did not cover those being transported at the time of the accident. Do not take chances. If necessary, take out a special insurance for the day rather than risk the high cost of damages in the event of an accident.

27. Give complete and accurate details of your fund-raising event to the public

When you advertise your event on radio, television or in newspapers, make sure that you give all the details about the event. Remember to give the date, time and place. It is surprising how often this vital information is missing from advertisements, and poor attendance is bound to result.

It is helpful to state the cost of admission and any other relevant details that you think will encourage people to attend your function rather than try somewhere else. People also like to know what special attractions await them if they take the trouble to attend.

It often helps to remind people about the aims and objectives of your group. It stimulates interest if you can tell the public why you need the money, how much you are hoping to raise, and what you are hoping to do with the profits. People are always keen to learn more about the charity to which they give their support.

Advertising is expensive, but it is important that the public learn all about your charity event. You cannot expect a good turnout if you have not told people all the facts that they need to know. If possible, find some way to cover the cost of advertising your event, but do not skimp on promoting your ventures to the public.

28. Notify the proper authorities when you hold special events

If you organise a balloon race, for example, and large quantities of balloons are to be released, you should notify the Civil Aviation Authority. This department will advise you where you can release the balloons and they will tell you how many can be released at any one time.

In one competition, 150,000 gas-filled balloons were sold. The prize was to be a holiday for two in Spain. All the contestants had to do was to write their name on a label, and the winner would be the person whose balloon was found the furthest distance away. In this instance, the aviation authorities directed that specified quantities of the balloons be released at hourly intervals so that they would not endanger air traffic. It took twelve hours to release all of the balloons, and they floated across the Continent to countries far and wide.

In different fund-raising events there will be other Government authorities that need to be kept informed and officials will give appropriate guidance and help.

29. Make sure that prices are fair

It is important to make enquiries to establish what is a fair rate to charge for an entry fee, a competition entry, or for the price of goods to be sold. If prices are too high you will lose custom, and if they are too low you will not gain an adequate profit.

Prices for any charity event must be clearly displayed for everyone to see and understand.

30. *Do not repeat mistakes that have been made in the past*

When the event is over, take time to analyse any problems that may have occurred. Do not leave it to untried members of a new fund-raising committee to find out the weak spots again the following year.

Do not delay holding an inquest on your big event. Talk about the positive and negative aspects while it is still fresh in the memory of all concerned. Helpers will have learned a lot from their experiences on the day, and they may have many helpful suggestions which will benefit future events. Make notes of all positive suggestions so that committee members in future years can make practical use of the ideas.

Some common (and very simple) mishaps that can be avoided might include the following problems:

☒ Insufficient numbers of pens.

☒ Inadequate supplies of pins, scrap paper, or lined paper (on which to write the names and addresses of persons entering competitions).

☒ Insufficient numbers of tickets, pamphlets, entry forms, application forms, posters and other administrative paraphernalia.

☒ Not getting sponsors well in advance of the event.

☒ Giving the wrong people responsible jobs to do, and not checking that the work has been done as requested. (For instance, if someone 'forgets' to collect a prize that has been offered, it can cause a lot of bad feeling all round!)

Learn from your mistakes and make sure that they are recorded so that the new committee can benefit from hindsight the following year. This will help to ensure an even more rewarding event next time.

31. Take precaution and guard against cheating and fraud

Of all the hazards and pitfalls to fund-raising, theft, fraud and cheating can do the most damage. These problems can totally destroy a group's credibility. Don't say 'It cannot happen to our group' because I have news for you: many apparently respectable and kind members have brought dishonour and shame to their cause.

In some cases that go to court, well-known people in public life have been convicted of embezzlement. Often they say they behaved dishonourably in an attempt to avert financial disaster for the charity group, but the sad fact remains that, once an organisation is convicted of fraud, it can never fully survive the aftermath of exposure.

Never ignore the possibility of frauds, cheats and thieves being amongst your most valued helpers and supporters. Do not leave temptation open to your members. If you become too complacent about such things, you may leave your group wide open to such abusive behaviour.

It is vital that your books are audited regularly by an approved accountant who will scrutinise all income and expenditure and draw attention to any deviations from normal. Publicise what you are doing openly, and face the public with a clear conscience. Let people see, hear and comprehend all that your group is doing at every stage in the game. If your group is trusted it will be given support, so do nothing that will diminish this trust.

Fund-raising groups must remember that they are responsible for the actions of their members. Both the law and the public will blame the group for the behaviour of the one deviant member. It is up to the group to ensure that all precautions are taken to ensure that thieves and villains are actively discouraged.

Do not sell goods under false pretences. Look inside boxes that are donated to ensure that the contents are as stated on the box.

It is illegal to sell home-made wine, spirits and beer at any charity function. The sale of alcohol requires a licence, even if it is only home-made plonk! If you want to sell these items, then persuade your local publican or wine bar manager to extend his licence so that he can sell wine, spirits and beer at your function quite legally.

Remind helpers to be on the alert for pickpockets and others who will try to cheat the group out of its profits in a variety of ways. People, sadly, are always looking for a chance to steal a purse, or to take an item from a counter without payment. Some people make quite a lucrative profit from cheating at competitions and games. Your group must never ignore the possibility of fraud, however minor, because if they are complacent and think it will never happen to them, they will not take the necessary precautions to avoid mishaps, and they will leave temptation for people to find.

Cheating, fraud and theft can cause a lot of ill feeling in a group. No one knows who to blame and, as a result, a happy day can turn into a disaster. There are many ways of cheating which can cause disruption to a group. Here are some of the most common offences, all of which can easily be overcome:

1. It is an offence to put a winning ticket to one side so that it cannot be drawn (for example, when running a tombola stall)

If the organisers want to keep the bottle of whisky until the end in order to persuade more people to buy tickets, they may be tempted to put aside the winning ticket. The local authority Trading Standards Officer will not be deterred from taking action because the money is being donated to charity or because the culprits were trying to benefit their cause. The Trading Standards Officer is employed to protect the public from fraud, and he will prosecute if he finds such flagrant disregard of the law- even if the action was done with the best intentions for the group.

2. Never sell spirits that have been watered down – this is a criminal offence

One incidence of this was at a fete run by a charity group that allowed another organisation to run an independent tombola stall at their event. Two members of the public complained that they believed they had won bottles of gin on a tombola stall, when instead the bottles contained water. The host charity denied that they knew anything about the 'doctored' gin and blamed the pub that had donated it. Naturally the pub's manager was deeply offended by these allegations and the local police were asked to intervene. They found that the pub had donated three bottles of gin, yet six people had won bottles as prizes on the stall. The truth was revealed: the people operating the tombola stall were so dis- appointed with their takings that they decided to fill the bottles with water to try to attract more customers. They had been so anxious to benefit their cause that they had not stopped to think they were cheating the public to gain their ends.

In this case, unthinking people also caused their host charity to come under suspicion. The charity lost all credibility in the area, and it was very soon disbanded. The group that ran the rogue tombola stall were more fortunate. A new committee took over the responsibility of organising fund-raising on its behalf and later raised money by more noble efforts.

3. Play the game fairly

A popular fund-raising game is to offer contestants a straw which contains a numbered raffle ticket. It is a game of chance, and the winner obviously picks a straw containing the winning number. This game is fun to play, and it can be a very good money spinner, especially if there are some exciting prizes to win. Unfortunately, there have been many occasions in past years when Trading Standards Officers have found no winning numbers at all amongst the straws being offered. On other occasions, the winning numbers had been put to one side so that 'dead' straws were being offered. The resulting prosecutions left the groups concerned feeling stunned and ashamed – especially as committee members were not aware that their helpers had cheated in this way.

The public must have an even chance of winning a prize. They must not be cheated out of a fair game. Always make sure that prizes are what they appear to be too! Check that seals are intact on bottles, because drinks must not be tampered with in any way. There have been occasions when home-made wine has been put into a spirits bottle with the original label left on to tempt people to buy tickets. This is a deliberate attempt to mislead the public, and it is a criminal offence.

The blame for discrepancies such as these must fall on the person who is in control. It is up to the person running the stall to make sure that people are getting a fair deal for their money.

4. The lottery ticket scandals

Lotteries have always been popular with the public, and they have proved to be an excellent way of making money for good causes. Unfortunately, they are all too frequently vulnerable to mismanagement by helpers who are more concerned with making money for their charity than in being fair to their public. Often the committees of fund-raising groups have no knowledge of the devious activities of misguided members, and yet it is the charity that suffers when criminal activity is exposed.

There are several ways in which lottery ticket sellers can cheat their public, but the Gaming and Lotteries Acts have done a great deal to protect and safeguard the public in this respect. It is up to each fund-raising group to take precautions to ensure that the laws regarding lottery tickets are adhered to for the benefit of all concerned. Always draw lottery and raffle tickets in a public place. Invite at least one prominent figure to witness the placing of the counterfoils into the drum, and to witness the thorough mixing of all the tickets.

One example of a lottery ticket scandal occurred in a very popular, well established country club. A sharp-eyed member who was a policeman became suspicious when he checked and found that it was always a close friend or a relative of a club employee who won the regular weekly raffle. When he looked inside the drum and inspected the winning raffle ticket, his suspicions were confirmed. The ticket had been stuck to the side of the drum with a piece of bluetac so that the person drawing the tickets always knew where to find it! He said nothing at the time, but surveillance by two policemen the following week revealed the same thing happening again, and two men were arrested. The club manager knew nothing about the activities of his employees but their actions affected the club very seriously. Later it was deprived of a licence for six months because it was held that management were responsible for the behaviour of its members.

Other cases of fraud could easily fill a book. Some of these have included: weighting, by the use of gum, on spinning wheels to affect their performance; injecting small amounts of water into table tennis balls to affect their performance; telling people the answers to puzzles and games in advance.

Some years ago, I devised a competition 'How long will it take for a three inch candle to burn?' Competitors had to guess the answer to the nearest tenth of a second. The group acted on my advice and ran a test candle so that they would have some idea when the competition candle would burn out. In this way they could ensure that a member of their group would be present at the right time.

Only nine people knew the time it took the test candle to burn. The actual competition was popular, and the variation in the guesses was enormous. All but one person was at least an hour out in his guess. The winner was only five minutes and nine seconds from the correct time.

In previous games, there had never been such a close guess as this, and I mentioned my disquiet to the secretary. At first he was annoyed by my implications, but he made some discreet enquiries and found that the winner was closely related to a member of his committee. When he visited the winner and told him of his suspicions, the man confessed. He had been told unofficially the time that the test candle took to go out, and he used this information as his guide.

In this case the man had been suffering from a terrible case of conscience, and he was glad that his action had come out into the open. The committee member was dismissed from any further connection with the group, and the competition was run a second time. The same entries were used, this time with a different thickness of candle, and the winner was chosen fairly. In spite of these efforts, it took the group a long time to live down the scandal, and it took some time for their fund-raising efforts to recover.

Human nature is unpredictable. Greed, jealousy, fear of financial hardship and failed ambition can promote devious activity from the most unlikely people. What is worse, if they succeed, and get away with it, they feel they have been given the licence to try again. If the problem goes undetected for a long time, the group will fall all the harder when the crimes are detected.

Your group must not be naive. It only needs one person to deviate from the straight and honest path, and the whole group is in trouble.

Part 2

CASE HISTORIES - PROBLEMS ENCOUNTERED BY FUND-RAISING GROUPS

The stories that follow illustrate many of the common problems encountered by fund-raising groups in their endeavours to make money for their cause. The case histories are factual, although some details about the type of groups and their geographical whereabouts have been changed.

By describing the experiences of others, I hope *not* to frighten readers, but to enable them to benefit from learning about the mistakes of others. Fund-raisers must be aware of the dangers if they are to take the correct steps to avoid them.

All fund-raising activities can provide pleasurable occupation. The hazards and pitfalls of fund-raising will only trap those who are not well informed of their existence. If certain precautions are taken, fund-raising can provide financial profit and a sense of personal achievement that make all the effort worthwhile.

Case 1 – THE DISCO

Even an experienced group, well qualified and capable of organising fund-raising projects, can make the wrong decisions when under pressure. This once happened to a local branch of a national fund-raising group whose members were all successful businessmen, working with the help of their wives.

The group wanted to raise £15,000 to buy a mini-bus for transporting young people to a training centre. At first, the fund-raising moved very slowly, with income from coffee mornings, jumble sales, cake sales and lotteries. These were all time-consuming efforts which brought small amounts of profit very gradually into the kitty. The slow progress resulted in a further dilemma. As the money in the kitty increased, so did the cost of the bus. Members felt that they were chasing their own tails and would never reach their goal. Wives and helpers grew tired of the demands being made on their time, and they were becoming increasingly impatient with the demands being made on their partners. A quick solution had to be found. Then someone suggested a disco.

The plan was to invite a top radio disc jockey who would draw in the crowds. In this way, the group thought it would reap a great profit from just the one major event. It seemed like the answer to their prayers – an easy solution which would be well worth the effort involved.

The cost of the hire of a hall suitable for a large audience was much higher than expected, as was the cost of the equipment they had to hire. Worse still, the DJ's fee was astronomical. Hopes were high, however, and with thoughts of all those people queuing to get in, and the large profits expected, they threw caution to the wind. Never mind! It was well worth the gamble.

Then came the crunch. The group had not thought about the effect of a major factory closure in their area. Unemployment was rife, and the entry fee of £10 per head was beyond the price that the youngsters could afford, even to see their favourite DJ. Older people were not interested in a disco, and the result was disaster.

The event was very poorly attended. The disc jockey was annoyed and the committee were very embarrassed. The group *lost* the best part of £2,000 by trying to run this event, and morale sank very low.

Unfortunately, none of the committee members had organised a disco before. Some of the members had never been to a disco or seen one in operation, so their knowledge of such an operation was limited to hearsay.

The DJ was richer, after receiving his fee, plus expenses, and the owners of the hall did well from the rent. Even the firm that hired the equipment was well satisfied by the deal. It was just the fund-raising committee members and the mini-bus project that suffered. The loss had to be paid from members' pockets because it is illegal to raise funds for money lost through unwise expenditure, even in the pro- motion of a charity venture, and a few salutary lessons were learned by all.

- Find a good leader, a person who is a competent organiser and who can motivate his helpers.

- Find someone who has had experience in running and organising a disco, and ask for their advice and guidance.

- Do some research to find what price will be acceptable to those you hope will support your event.

- Work out the total costs involved, and decide how these costs are to be met.

- Find out what mobile discos there are in your area. They are advertised in the Yellow Pages or in the local press. If possible, check their reputation with other groups that have used them. Well-known personalities may appeal to those with a lot of money to spend, but local groups can provide an excellent evening of entertainment for a reasonable fee, and the music they play is the great attraction.

- If you are new to disco music, get a member of your group to talk to young people at a youth club or other meeting place, or amongst friends and family. Ask what kind of music they would enjoy. Find out from these young people whether they would support such a venture. These days, there is such a wide range of disco styles – all of which appeal to different groups of people. The popular TV image of thunderous music, incessant beat, strobe lighting, liberal use of drugs and frenetic dancing is not the only way of doing it.

- Seek a sponsor to cover the cost of printing tickets. In return you can offer to advertise his company on the ticket.

- Sell the tickets well in advance of the event. This will enable you to call off the venture at an early stage if ticket sales are not going well.

- When booking a hall, endeavour to have a provisional booking accepted. If you are offered a period between the provisional date offered and your confirmation of this date, then you lose only your provisional booking fee if you need to cancel the event.

- Make sure that you have sufficient helpers to take care of all eventualities on the night.

- Use the venue for organising a few games and competitions to raise more funds on the night.

- Sell refreshments.

- Find local sponsors to hire the disco, pay for the hall or to hire necessary equipment. Local firms who want to advertise the product they sell or the service they offer might be happy to help in some way in return for your promoting their business at the event. If you can find industry, shops, pubs or professional agencies to pay major costs, then your expenses are resolved before the event takes place, and every penny that you take on the night will go to your cause. You would not make a loss even if half of your anticipated number did not turn up! Most important: if you can find sponsorships you will suffer no disaster to thwart and demoralise your fund-raising group.

- Adequate advertising and promotion of a fund-raising event is very often forgotten. Many a well planned project is doomed to failure because the general public know nothing about the venture. It is important to use all the outlets available in order to advertise your event in advance.

Armed with answers to all the above questions, you can work out whether or not it will be practical to run a disco. In some areas they can be very popular. Do bear in mind that groups of people other than pop-conscious teenagers like disco too. They have often been a great success when organised specifically for those who like to dance to Elvis Presley, music of the 1950s, 1960s, 1970s or country. Many successful discos have been run where the organisers promised not to play the music at ear-splitting levels all night – some people like to dance and bop away to a quieter beat! If you do the basic research, as outlined, then you will know prior to the event whether you will make enough money from the venture to make it a success. Don't spend money on launching a project unless you are certain that you can justify the expense and effort involved.

Case 2 – A FETE

A local playgroup had tried many fund-raising ideas to try to raise money to purchase much needed equipment for their young members. Progress was slow and discouraging because none of their efforts had been very remunerative and, again, the prices of the items required had doubled since their efforts began two years before.

Committee members despaired of reaching their goal. They were ready to quit and close down the playgroup, but decided on one last attempt to put it on a sound financial footing. They would organise a fete. In their enthusiasm to raise a lot of money in one big event, they took none of the precautions that they should have done to avoid losing money. Common sense left the room and they began desperate measures to fulfil their dreams.

The committee decided to hire a large field to accommodate the crowds. In case it was wet, they would also hire two large marquees and they would fit various stalls all around the marquees and hold competitions and games that offered good prizes. A local football team offered the group the use of their ground for a fee of £80. A hire firm erected two marquees, and another firm filled the marquee with hired trestle tables. The committee were staggered by the cost of hiring this equipment, but they anticipated that this large slice from their financial resources would be easily recouped from big profits on the day.

Sadly, the committee members were unimaginative and they provided no interesting competitions to encourage people to spend their money. The atmosphere was dead and, worst still, the ground was situated in a most inaccessible place where there was parking for only twelve cars. This situation caused chaos, but perhaps it was lucky from the car parking point of view that the event had not been well advertised. Local people did not know that the event was being held, and so attendance was very poor.

The event was a soul-destroying experience for the committee members, and the group lost more than £600. It was the last straw. Members were defeated and the group split up altogether. The playgroup ceased to function and the equipment was never bought.

Children were denied an important extra dimension to their lives because of the inexperience and lack of planning of their fund-raising committee.

It should never have happened. The idea was a good one. It was just its method of execution that was wrong. Garden fetes have always been good money spinners (although I think the name 'garden fete' is outmoded and dull; I would prefer to call it something more exciting like gala festival or gala carnival day). Groups that decide upon an important event like this must exercise a great deal of planning, thought and effort to make it work.

- If the group felt that the weather was too unpredictable for the time of year, it could have found some way to recoup at least some part of the cost of hiring the marquee.

- The committee should have remembered that marquees have poles to support the outer walls. From these poles banners can be suspended – advertising banners, from which a good income can be obtained.

- Across the top of the marquee, between the two main poles, another large banner could be strung to be seen for miles around.

- If it had not been possible to find a sponsor to pay the cost of the marquee hire, the advertising banners would have met this cost. The group could easily receive a fee of £25 for each of the twelve banners round the outer walls; £20 for each of the banners inside the tent; and £50 for the large banner on top of the tent because of its prominent display.

- Many groups seem to skimp on the advertising of their events. Posters should have been displayed in supermarkets, newsagents, libraries, shops, and in any public place where permission can be obtained. People also look in the 'What's On' column in local newspapers to learn about local events.

- There are organisations willing to supply printed posters to advertise a big event. In return, your group would be asked to permit the name of its sponsor to be printed across the bottom of the poster.

- Display your posters at least 2-3 weeks prior to the event. This will give people time to make any necessary arrangements to attend.

- Sometimes it is possible to advertise an event free of charge on the radio, television and in the news media. Take advantage of any perks such as this, but do not wait until the day before the event before you advertise. This does not give people time to plan in advance. Quite often we hear details of a fund-raising event that is already in progress somewhere. How many people do these groups really think will be ready to turn out at a moment's notice to support a worthwhile cause that they know little about?

- With a little ingenuity, the stalls and competitions can give good value for money. Offer an exciting challenge and people will soon lose their shyness when they see others queuing up to play. If the competition or game is sufficiently interesting, you are bound to attract custom.

- As a bonus, encourage helpers to be cheerful and out-going. A friendly extrovert can inspire people with the enthusiasm to 'have a go' and your group cannot fail to succeed.

- Invite radio, television and press reporters to attend your event because this gives extra publicity to your cause.

A different approach to a gala carnival day

This is a name for a garden fete with a difference. The title 'garden fete' sounds dull and weary. People are looking for something exciting and different to occupy themselves during their leisure time, and I believe that Gala Carnival Day conjures up a party spirit, and it is a happy party atmosphere that you are trying to achieve.

Fancy dress

Invite members of the public to arrive in fancy dress – the more outlandish the better. As an extra incentive you can offer a really worthwhile prize for the most original male and female costume both for children and for adults. Also have a family costume entry section. You will be amazed at the response you will get. People love dressing up, and they love to see others in fancy costumes. A £1 fee can be charged for entry into the competition.

Do not miss the opportunity of selling entry tickets well in advance of the event. People are more likely to turn up, even on a cold, wet day, if they have already purchased their entry ticket. Even if they do not attend, the group is the richer for £1 for every person who bought a ticket and who did not attend. Those who purchase tickets in advance can also be offered a free entry into a small competition (perhaps the advertising competition mentioned on page 19). The prize for this event should be obtained from sponsorship if possible.

Sponsorship for prizes should be easy to get if you invite local radio, television and newspaper reporters and photographers to cover the event. To obtain sponsorship, you could make a concession and call your event: 'The Johnson and Phillips Gala Carnival Day'. In return, you would receive a large fee from Johnson and Phillips for advertising their firm. Alternatively, find manufacturers who will sponsor your event by allowing your helpers to wear some form of advertising garment – like arm bands or tabards – with printed advertising slogans.

Better still, if your sponsor markets, say tinned food, make up costumes which look like massive cans of beans or soup, and which bear the brand name of your sponsor. These will be popular with the public and with the advertiser. Such 'cans' can easily be made from cardboard boxes which you will find at your local supermarket, and they can be made very colourful and amusing. It is bound to improve your chance of getting support from a sponsor because he knows that his name and product are bound to be noticed.

If there are schools in your area, devise a fancy dress inter-schools competition. The children can enter in teams to depict nursery rhyme themes, historic events, or some current news theme. The prize could be a donation to the Parent Teachers Association fund, which would provide an extra incentive for teachers to encourage their children to enter the competition. The school with the most original team costume idea will win funds to buy special equipment that the PTA group might need for the school.

Carnival princess

Another popular competition is to judge a Carnival Princess and her attendants. Young girls between the ages of six and ten years love to dress up in the flowing gowns of a fairy princess. The vehicle used to transport the princess and her attendants can be decorated to show them off to best advantage. Attendants can be dressed beautifully, in a manner to complement the princess, and the vehicle can be fitted with special effects to make an appropriate setting for a fairy queen.

A small country village can make this a very exciting event by making it a district competition, with village A competing with villages B and C. Before the carnival begins, the cars carrying the princesses can be driven in a convoy along a pre-selected route.

The choice of the fairy princess and the judging of all other events should wait until at least half-way through the carnival as this ensures that the contestants and audience have plenty of time to look around the stalls and spend their money.

Make sure that your helpers retain their party atmosphere throughout the gala, perhaps by getting them also to wear fancy dress. They should encourage people to come to the stalls and explain the rules of the games so that people will want to try their luck. Helpers who are shy and embarrassed and lack confidence in what they are trying to do will not be an asset to the group. Helpers MUST be friendly and cheerful so that they inspire the public with happiness and joy.

It is most important to ensure that the stalls and competitions are lively and entertaining. If games provide a challenge and they are exciting to play, your helpers should have no trouble in drawing in the crowds to 'try their luck'.

Use the ideas for competitions and games from the wide selection in this book. You will also be able to devise new, fascinating games for yourself from ordinary day-to-day occurrences. One easy example is to ask contestants how long it would take for the bus to reach the carnival grounds from its depot. It is not as easy as it sounds, because there are all sorts of unexpected occurrences that cause times to be different on each outing. The winner is the person who guesses the time to the nearest second of the actual time.

Case 3 – THE AUTUMN FAIR

A group was raising funds to build an extension for a day centre for elderly people but found that the usual run of jumble sales and bring-and-buy stalls did not bring in the money that they needed quickly enough. The facilities were badly needed, and so the committee called a special meeting to try to think of ways of raising the necessary cash.

They agreed to hold a big Autumn Fair, and to draw in the crowds, they decided to invite a well-known television personality who was very popular and whom they knew would attract local people. For a large fee, the TV personality agreed to open the Fair, but as so often happens, very little effort had been made to publicise the event, apart from three posters placed in a pub, a newsagent and a corner shop. No other form of advertising was attempted. Presumably the committee felt that people were psychic and that they would learn about the event without being notified!

The event was a disaster. The committee had not taken into account the number of entry fees that would be needed to cover the cost of the television personality. They had to clear this debt before any profits could be made, and of course this was not possible with a poor turnout of people. Popular personalities may increase a big event considerably if it is well advertised. In most cases, however, their presence does not cover the extra expenses involved. In this case, the group covered their loss by money they had raised by other means, and so were able to meet their debts without bad publicity.

Luckily this group were willing to learn by their mistakes. With help and encouragement, they organised a second event, and this time they did not need to pay out one single penny. They made a considerable profit and thus made a handsome contribution to the start of the building extension, which now is fully completed.

The advice was that already outlined often in this book: avoid the hazards and pitfalls of fund-raising by **taking all the necessary precautions**.

Case 4 – A JUMBLE SALE

A Midlands-based silver band wanted to equip their members with new uniforms and decided to hold a jumble sale to raise the necessary funds. They booked a hall near the centre of town, and distributed leaflets to over 1,000 homes requesting jumble for the event. It was an enterprising group, and their helpers were very enthusiastic in their efforts, but unfortunately they made several common mistakes which proved fatal.

First they forgot to make enquiries to find out whether there were other similar schemes being held on the same day. As it happened, there were *seven* other fund-raising groups holding a jumble sale in the same area and at around the same time, and all the houses in the district were approached by all eight groups for jumble. The group did its best, and collected jumble from the homes of its faithful followers and friends; the other charities had to be content with what was left over.

Parking facilities also caused problems for this venture because the only place to park was in a multi-storey carpark nearby. This was expensive and inaccessible to the hall, and so would-be customers were discouraged from attending the jumble sale. Only the friends and relatives of the band made the effort to support the group.

It was an expensive day for the silver band. They had realised some money on the entry fee of 25p and on the sale of the jumble, but it was not enough to pay the cost of hiring the hall, printing pamphlets and hiring trestle tables. If members had included the cost of petrol for cars used in collecting the jumble, their loss would have been greater.

After all this, there was still the task of disposing of a lot of rubbish that had been left over. They had not thought to sell the old clothing to a dealer for a few extra pounds.

It was a sad group that realised its errors too late. If each member of the group had contributed only £2 the band would have been well into profit and the members would have been saved a lot of hard work and wasted time.

Case 5 – A POP FESTIVAL

A charity group wishing to raise funds for cancer research decided on a very ambitious project. They would hold a pop festival in the hope of attracting people from all over the British Isles. It was agreed that the event would be run over an entire weekend, and elaborate plans were made to launch the project in the hope of a massive profit.

Sadly, the organisers made many of the usual mistakes. The land they chose was not easily accessible to the public. The charges were too high. The event was not well advertised, and the venture ran into a lot of problems.

Some of the artists charged exorbitant fees. The cost of hiring marquees and other equipment was high, and as none of the organisers had previously been involved in a venture like this, they did not know of the likely pitfalls. They hoped to recoup their losses, but they did not take the trouble to find out how to run a big event like this effectively.

The result was an eventual disaster. The group lost £25,000 and many small businessmen faced financial ruin.

Pop festivals in the right situation can be very profitable, but there are a lot of pitfalls. To run a smooth operation and make a profit, you need careful planning and administration.

First it is necessary to make enquiries into the feasibility of the site that has been chosen. In some neighbourhoods, the local population has caused so much friction and opposition that the proposed festival has had to be abandoned. People are afraid of all the negative aspects that must be considered and dealt with appropriately. Unfortunately, history shows that many such festivals do encourage bad behaviour and the media pounce on this with glee and spread the news everywhere. The image is often therefore one of hooliganism, drugs, riots, thefts, vandalism and sexual offences, not to mention the fear of noise, pollution of the countryside and general mess and devastation of the area. The fact that the music was brilliant is often overlooked.

Once you have found a good site, it is necessary to make enquiries from the local authority. You need to gain planning permission to stage a big event that may attract thousands of people.

Make sure that landowners are willing to take the risk of damage to fences or crops in the area surrounding the site. It is better to chose a site that is surrounded by grassland because no insurance company will insure against damage at a pop festival. Your group is likely to have to pay the cost of damages out of its own funds.

Pop festivals are very expensive to organise and run. It is best to seek the sponsorship of a big company that can help to finance the venture. Cigarette firms in need of new advertising outlets may be glad to use the venue for advertising as they have been denied many other outlets by the present laws regarding tobacco advertising. Drinks firms, banks and other industries often seek opportunities to advertise and promote themselves in big ventures like this. If you cannot find a sponsor, it would be best to cancel the idea altogether rather than risk losing a lot of cash.

Pop festivals tend to appeal to a certain age group, and it is up to your group to ensure that there are sufficient numbers of enthusiasts living within a few miles' radius of your festival. Employ the services of a person who has had knowledge of the pop scene. He or she will negotiate the bookings of pop groups and advise you which groups should be invited to play at your event.

It is important to provide adequate fresh water and toilet facilities, refreshment areas, food stalls and bars. You may also decide to invite certain market stalls to operate at the venue. Your group must have a host of willing helpers to undertake the multitude of tasks needed to make an ambitious project like this a success.

Case 6 – LOTTERIES

Small lotteries can be very vulnerable, especially if the prizes are to be purchased with money raised in the venture. People need the attraction of substantial prizes before they show any great interest in buying lottery tickets, and if the prize is to be set at, say, £300 or more, the group has to find either a sponsor or a way of selling sufficient tickets to pay for the cost of the prizes and the printing of tickets.

This objective is frequently not achieved. One group I know fell into the trap of organising a lottery at the same time as several other charities who were each holding a similar event. It was Christmas, and that year there were nineteen organisations all holding their lottery draw in the same week in December. Several of the draws were held on the same day. Eleven out of the nineteen lotteries lost money, two managed to break even, and the remaining six, which had offered substantial prizes and were able to secure greater ticket sales, made a reasonably handsome profit for their cause.

One unfortunate group disbanded soon after the catastrophe. It had been trying to raise money for a hostel for disabled people, but committee members were so discouraged by the poor response to their efforts that they forked out the money from their own pockets to recoup losses, and opted out of the scheme. They did not dare risk a repeat of financial disaster.

Another cause of problems in a lottery competition is poor distribution of tickets. Some groups have developed the bad habit of leaving lottery books on counters in pubs or retail shops. They hope that customers will see the tickets and buy them! Anyone who believes that this is an efficient way to sell tickets is living in a dream world. Very few people will notice the tickets, and if they do see them, they would not be inspired to buy one without a little encouragement and persuasion from a sales person.

Remember, members of the public like to see professional-looking posters that give details of the lottery and the prizes to be won.

In one case, a newsagent which sold 6,400 newspapers and magazines a week sold only 27 lottery tickets after a two-week period.

As the cost of the tickets was only 25p, the charity learned its lesson not to leave the sale of lottery tickets to chance again. Only people with time to linger and contemplate which paper to buy had even noticed the lottery tickets on the counter.

Landlords in pubs do not usually like to sell lottery tickets because they have no time to give them due attention and there is a chance that the money will be stolen. In one bar, tickets and money were left in a pint mug to attract customers: the mug was stolen, together with the counterfoils. In this instance, the names of people who had paid for tickets were not known, and so they were not likely to win a prize. This is quite illegal. Everyone who buys a ticket must have an even chance of winning.

A poor selection of prizes can be another reason for lottery failures. Many prizes hold no interest whatsoever to the person buying the ticket, and this can be a real disaster. It pays to be imaginative and choose prizes that will appeal to most people. A Christmas turkey is a popular prize, but not if people have to wait until five days before Christmas before the prize is drawn; most people order their turkey in advance.

Some imaginative prizes could include the following:

🏆 The hire of a car for three months from a local car hire firm.

🏆 A voucher for 150 litres of free petrol from a local garage.

🏆 Eight free meals at a good local restaurant (to be taken over a period of three months).

🏆 Cosmetics to the value of £50 from a local store.

🏆 Four free hair appointments, taken over a four-month period.

🏆 Six free driving lessons from a local driving school.

You need the assistance of a host of willing and reliable helpers to sell lottery tickets. Enthusiastic sales talk will encourage people to buy the tickets, but if members of your group look upon this task as a chore they are unlikely to sell many tickets. It is more likely that they will purchase the tickets for themselves, or return most of their tickets unsold.

If you do *not* put on sale tickets valued at more than £20,000 for a lottery, or for more than £250,000 in any given calendar year, is important to register your lottery with the Local Authority before you organise the event. (Ticket sales over these amounts demands registration with the Gaming Board.) Failure to do this will make your group liable to prosecution, which results in bad publicity and can prove disastrous to a charity. During the past few years, I have known at least thirty groups that had forgotten to register their lotteries, and in each case the police were asked to investigate their activities. Even though the lotteries were for vital community needs, the police were left with no alternative but to prosecute the groups. The Gaming and Lotteries Acts have been in existence for many years, and ignorance about their existence cannot be accepted as a viable excuse.

The Gaming and Lotteries Acts were made to protect the public from mismanagement of money by unscrupulous organisations, and to prevent commercial enterprises from using lotteries for monetary gain. Groups that fail to obey the laws may be liable to appearance in court, heavy fines, and bad publicity. The groups I mentioned had to refund all monies received from contestants and also pay the cost of printing the tickets and organising the event from members' pockets. This caused a great deal of embarrassment to the groups concerned, as well as real financial hardship. If they had applied for a licence, and proved that they were running a lottery for charity and for a worthwhile cause, they would not have run into difficulties and they could have been very successful.

Your local authority will be able to supply you with a simple leaflet describing the requirements for local societies, on matters such as registration, conduct of lotteries, management, returns and pool betting. Read these notes carefully.

Case 7 – THE SPONSORED WALK

A community group once decided to organise a sponsored walk to raise funds for its centre. More than one hundred people agreed to participate in the belief that they would suffer the experience for the benefit of others.

Unfortunately, the group were faced with the usual hazards that beset this type of venture. First the public were not enthusiastic about paying the participants money for each mile they managed to walk. They were uninspired by the promise to walk from A to B, and only small pledges of money were achieved. The maximum amount sponsored was £10. The walkers were subjected to training in treacherous weather, and their aching feet and leg muscles were suffered for nothing.

People did not always honour the promised amounts. The result was very little profit for their cause, and a great deal of discontent and frustration by members.

With one hundred participants, just think of what could have been achieved if the event had been organised properly, or if the committee had devoted their efforts to something a little more enterprising and worthwhile.

If you want to do a sponsored walk, then make it a walk with a difference. A project like this must give pleasure and entertainment to both contestants and members of the public, if it is to succeed. If the event will amuse, entertain or benefit the public in some way, then it has a lot more chance of making money and doing good for your cause.

To make your sponsored walk exciting, and to raise substantial sums of money for your cause, try some of the following tips:

- Encourage your walkers to give you a written guarantee of their participation. This gives people some moral obligation to honour their promise to take part in the event, and, more The Complete Guide to Fund-Raising importantly, it gives you an idea of how many people will be taking part in the sponsored walk on the day.

- With this information, seek sponsorship from large national firms as well as from local business. In return for their financial support, you can offer to advertise their product or service during the walk. Contestants will be asked to wear armbands, sashes or items of clothing that bear the name of the product the manufacturer wants to sell.

- Better still, if the manufacturer really wants to draw attention to his product, he will be happy to sponsor your venture if you offer to have two walkers carry an enormous cardboard model of his product with the name of the manufacturer printed clearly for all to see. Some examples are as follows:

  - If you seek sponsorship from a retail shoe shop, offer to have two people wear a large model of two shoes around their necks bearing the name of the shop (see Figure 2).

  - If a taxi firm wants to advertise its services, a model taxi could be made, one half tied to the person on the left and the other half to a partner by his side.

  - If you have a newsagent as a sponsor, dress two people in suits made of newspapers, and give them a large placard bearing the name of the sponsor.

There is no limit to the fancy dress variations that you can achieve. All this will encourage firms to sponsors your event and it will make the walk more entertaining and fun to watch for spectators. If you have one hundred walkers, and you get £30 for each pair of walkers from sponsors, you will have earned £1,500 for your cause before the competition begins. All monies raised by walkers after that will be a bonus.

When planning a sponsored walk, make sure that you advise your local authority about the venture, and also notify and gain permission for the walk from the police. In this way you will avoid running into problems on route! The police have a duty to ensure that the roads are free from hazards both for motorists and for the general public, so if the route that you have chosen is unsuitable, you may be asked to make changes. Don't leave the route planning until too late, when spectators and helpers might be waiting in the wrong places.

Good relationships with the police, the local authority, and with local firms, pubs and landowners are essential to happy and successful fund raising.

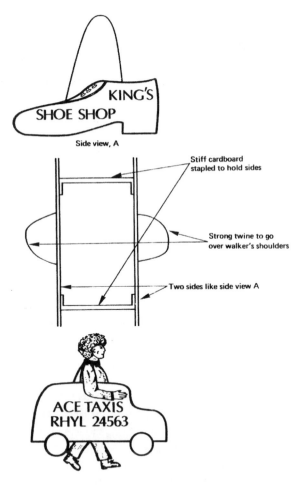

Figure 2 – Sponsorship placards

Case 8 – FUND-RAISING FOR A DRAMA GROUP

I once received a call for help from a theatrical group while I was doing a phone-in programme on the radio. This group had tried to raise £42,000 for two years to buy a small theatre in their home town. They had found a suitable property and the owners had agreed to wait a maximum of 2½ years for the group to find the funds to pay for it. Sadly their time was running out, and the owner had refused to extend the period of time offered.

There were sixteen members of the group, but none had prior experience in fund-raising, and they had no idea how to raise the large amount of money needed. They did not want to lose the property because the cost of alternative buildings was rising fast, while this property price was being held for them.

The group's members had great ambitions, but little fund-raising talent, and their efforts had been devoted to holding coffee mornings. Every day of the week, except Sunday, one of the committee members would hold a coffee morning in her home, and a raffle plus the sale of cakes, jumble, craft and books to boost the profits. In spite of these efforts, each member could rarely expect to make much profit, and at the end of two years their income reached only £1,560 towards the cost of the new theatre!

When I met the group committee and explained that it needed careful planning of special events to raise such a large sum of money, they were a little apprehensive. I gave them a selection of games and competitions, some of which are outlined in this book, and explained how each event should be executed. Much encouraged, they recommended their fund-raising efforts with new enthusiasm. They made such good progress, that the property owner agreed to extend the time allowed to pay for the property, and triumphantly they managed to raise the money within twelve days of their six months' deadline.

Another theatre group was not so lucky. It had begun raising funds for a specially adapted mini-bus, but after twelve months its cost had risen so much that they were still far from achieving their objective. The group were devoid of any sensible fund-raising ideas, and they did not know how to interest local businessmen in their project. Their most ambitious effort was a Christmas Fair, but as this only comprised seven stalls in a very small hut, the profit of £176 was perhaps more than they deserved. The group made no efforts to seek outside help, and they finally abandoned the project and devoted their voluntary efforts to other endeavours.

There are three **golden rules** to consider if your group needs to make money quickly:

1. *Good planning activity* **is essential.**

2. **Choose a major fund-raising project that will *earn money quickly,* rather than many small events that are time-consuming.**

3. **Set yourself a *target date* to accomplish the figure you need, and make your members promise to give maximum time and effort to the project during this period.**

Case 9 – THE YOUTH CLUB

Many groups fail to plan their events in advance, and this is one of the pitfalls that can easily be avoided. Unexpected delays can occur in the most well planned fund-raising activity, but if the group has given itself time to offset holdups in administration, delays will not cause any serious problem.

Printers are a main culprit in this respect, I am afraid. They can be very misleading with their promises of delivery dates as they tend to look after their bigger customers first. This is understandable, and it makes good sense to the printer, but not so to a charity that has fixed the dates of a competition. If tickets and posters are not ready on time, there may be serious consequences. For example, I know of one group that received its entry forms for a competition three days after the closing date of the event. The game could not even be started.

Another group received its printed forms just six days prior to the closing date of a fund-raising competition that was to have lasted three weeks. It took the leader one and a half days to distribute all the tickets to helpers, and there was hardly any time left to ensure a financial success for the project. Only 106 people entered the competition and the income received barely covered the cost of printing and administration. If the leader had recovered petrol costs for delivering the tickets, then the venture would have made a loss.

Another common dilemma is when the group is presented with an unacceptable printer's error. The forms then have to be reprinted, and the delays can cause havoc to a group that has not given itself time to cope with such an emergency.

This problem caused the downfall of a fund-raising group that was holding a Christmas bazaar. The printer had omitted to print vital information on the posters, and so these had to be reprinted. By the time they were ready, there were only three days left to display them. This group were in further trouble because they were depending solely on the posters to advertise their event and had little or no time to advertise it in any other way. The result was very poor attendance at a bazaar that had otherwise been very well organised, and the members were lucky to break even.

Delay in printing can also cause problems if there is insufficient time for competitors to follow the rules of the game. For instance, if people are asked to collect tokens or join a treasure trail, they will need time to accomplish this. They will not pay to enter a competition if the closing date is too near.

Allow eight or nine weeks for printing and then you will not have problems caused by delays in obtaining your printed matter in good time before the event. It is best to be in possession of printed documents at least a month before they are needed. Depending on the qualities of printed material you need, it is sometimes better to visit a copy-shop and wait while the work is being done. This is best achieved during the slack part of the day, if one of your committee members is free.

Lack of time can cause other problems. It sometimes takes longer than expected to find good sponsors. It is important to find the right firm, so start looking for sponsors three or four months prior to the event if possible. Give yourself plenty of time.

Volunteer helpers are not always dependable and work often has to be reallocated to other members of the group. This can cause hold-ups and delay the start of a project if a lot of work is involved, so be prepared for eventualities like this. Don't let lack of time spoil the efficient organisation and administration of fund-raising events.

Case 10 – THE FISHING COMPETITION

Fishing competitions can be great fun, but poor administration and bad weather can jeopardise proceedings, and then the often poor communications between the organisers and fishermen can ruin the occasion for all concerned. Only if you have experience in this area and your group has access to private fishing grounds can you really be sure of reducing the hazards of a fishing competition to a minimum. Even then, the weather plays such an important part that the work involved in organising the event may not be worth the low profits achieved.

One fund-raising group I know decided to run a fishing competition in order to raise funds for a research project. They secured 238 entries for the competition, each paying a £1 entry fee. A sports shop that sold fishing tackle sponsored one of the prizes.

Two days prior to the contest, a violent storm erupted and torrential rains swept the countryside for over thirteen hours. The river bank chosen for the competition was flooded and the gushing waters swamped many acres of field. The organisers could not contact the fishermen in time, and most contestants arrived on the day to find that fishing had been abandoned. There was no alternative venue within twenty miles that would have been suitable.

A new date was later arranged, but this proved a bad choice as contestants had already scheduled for other competitions far and wide. Four alternative dates were chosen, and the cost of postage and stationery soared. Finally the event was cancelled, and the entry fees and sponsored prizes were returned.

Fishing events are best left to those who are used to organising them because they have a better chance of success.

Case 11 – INSURANCE FOR INJURY

Accidents happen at the most unexpected times, and they can have a devastating effect on fund-raising groups.

A group in Manchester organised a Wellington boot throwing competition as an added fun attraction in their garden fete. I suggested that they take out insurance against third party injury and to seek a sponsor who would pay for the premium, but they had held the event twice previously with no mishap and so insisted that it was not worth the effort involved. They were trying to raise funds for facilities for disadvantaged children, and as this was a worthwhile cause, they felt confident that no one would sue them for a minor injury.

The wellie throwing game is a lot of fun, and spectators like to watch people try to throw the bulky objects. On this occasion a big crowd had gathered to watch, and they laughed appreciatively as a very plump man tried to throw the wellie in the right direction. He gave his third wellie a mighty swing and it shot out of his hand and hit a woman spectator full force in the eye. People watched in horror as the top of her eye was split open and the blood began to spurt.

The unfortunate woman was taken to hospital and detained for over three weeks as doctors tried to save the sight of her eye. The stitches had scarred her face and she sued the organisation that ran the fete. Her problem was exacerbated because her eyesight was impaired and, as she needed good sight for her job, she was forced to resign. Two years after the accident, the court awarded her a substantial sum in damages against the fund-raising group that had organised the event. The onus to pay this debt fell on the nineteen members of the committee. One member had to sell his car, and another took out a second mortgage on his home to pay his share.

No one could have foreseen a disaster like this happening, but it is always best to take out insurance, just in case. Some insurance companies will cover an event if it gives prominent advertising for the firm, and it is well worth the effort to seek such an offer.

It is almost impossible to take precautions to ensure that no accidents ever occur. Many strange things happen, like the sudden explosion of an electric light bulb that was suspended over a stall at a fete. The hall was plunged into darkness, and fragments of glass shattered and forcefully struck the face of a young man who was standing at the stall. He was taken to hospital in terrible pain and shock, and five pieces of glass were removed from his cheeks and forehead after surgery. Many months later, this man was left with three small scars that marred his good looks. He was awarded a claim for thousands of pounds by the courts, much to the horror of the fund-raising group. Luckily in this case a local businessman paid the debt on behalf of the charity.

Many equally unlucky occurrences have shocked and stunned spectators, but although they may have done nothing more serious than frighten people, the organising groups have learned to insure against all accidents that might happen at future events.

Case 12 – THE SWIMMING CONTEST AND QUIZ EVENT

Before embarking on a particular fund-raising venture, make sure that it will gain support in your area. Many groups take a chance, without making preliminary enquiries to find out if people are interested in the type of event that they have in mind.

For example, there was one occasion when a fund-raising group tried to run a cycle rally in a district inhabited mainly by retired people; of course, there were few entries. Jumble sales are sometimes held in areas unsuited to this type of event. It is vital to do a little research into the feasibility of a fund-raising project in a particular location. Choose events that attract the local population.

Groups that choose inappropriate projects have long suffered for their folly, but failure to organise and communicate properly with people can also have dire consequences, as shown by a small group in the south of England who tried to raise funds for a recreation centre by organising a swimming gala.

They invited the heads of all schools within a radius of fifteen miles to enter teams of children to swim against famous swimming personalities. The response seemed good, and the group went ahead with their plans without waiting for written acceptances from the schools. They took it for granted that teachers would arrange for the children to attend. Communications were so bad that the children did not learn about the gala, and on the night of the special event, only seven swimmers arrived to compete, and only sixteen spectators came to watch. Luckily, the swimming personalities were sympathetic and they waived their fees, but the group learned a very sad lesson at a loss of £350.

The first mistake this group made was not to insist upon written confirmation on how many pupils were interested in competitive swimming, and how many entries there would be on the day. Secondly, they should have sold tickets in advance of the event, and then they would have known exactly how many people to cater for on the night. They should have also checked that the swimming gala did not clash with any other major inter-school event. This group were so confident of the success of their venture that the members did not take any of the normal precautions to ensure that the event would be well supported.

Always do some research into whether your idea for a fund-raising venture is as attractive to others as you think it will be. If it gets verbal support, then encourage participants to send in written confirmation of their intentions to take part. An enterprising fund-raising group in South Wales learned this lesson when they tried to organise a quiz contest to raise funds for animal welfare. They sent out invitations to twelve pubs, and anticipated that each would find a team of five keen quiz enthusiasts to take part in the first heats. The finals were to take place in a hall that would accommodate 500 people, each paying 50p to watch the final rounds of the game. Each team were to have paid an entry fee and, with raffles, the group hoped to raise more than £1,000.

Too late, the group found that regulars in only two of the pubs were interested in taking part, and in one they could not even raise a full team of five. The event had to be cancelled, and as local radio, television and newspapers had offered to give the competition news coverage and support, this caused the group a great deal of embarrassment, and a loss of £250 in administrative costs for an event that never happened.

Quizzes are a good idea for a fund-raising scheme, as they can prove very popular, but an event like this will only be successful if sufficient people want to take part. If members of the committee had taken the time to encourage people to participate and if they had enlisted the support of the pubs' landlords and staff, their efforts would have been justly rewarded.

Take nothing for granted. If only people would organise their fund-raising schemes as efficiently as they organise their home and business enterprises, they would be saved a great deal of heartache and hard work!

Case 13 – CAR BOOT SALES

Car boot sales are a very popular fund-raising gimmick. If organised efficiently, they can provide a useful income, but unfortunately this type of event is vulnerable to problems that can have dire consequences for the fund-raising group.

Many groups are tempted to hold a car boot sale without giving the project any real planning and thought. One group, trying to raise funds for an animal sanctuary, decided to try this event. They hired a field and invited people to bring their own second-hand goods for sale. The income for the group was a £5 fee for every car that used the facilities they offered.

Unfortunately, the event attracted market traders who found the fee cheaper than hiring a stall in the market. They had hoped to escape detection by the local authority inspectors, but they were recognised and charged with selling goods on a Sunday, and selling shoddy goods. Furthermore, as traders cannot trade without a licence, they were prosecuted for all three offences.

Sadly, the fund-raising group were also charged. Their offence was to contravene the Sunday trading laws, and this caused them a great deal of embarrassment. They were also held responsible for the sale of shoddy goods that had been purchased by the unsuspecting public. The inspectors were very sympathetic to the charity concerned, but they could not charge the traders only. Laws are made to include everyone.

Hold car boot sales on any day but a Sunday. This may reduce attendances, but better this than face prosecution. Market traders are discouraged from operating on weekdays when their stalls are in operation, and this is some consolation.

Case 14 – HORSE RACING

Many magazines offer advertisements for the hire of video tapes of horse-racing events; projectors can also be hired to show the horses racing across the screen. Charitable groups have been tempted to hire these videos for an evening, without taking the necessary legal precautions. They charge an entry fee and raise extra money by inviting people to gamble on the races in the same way as they would in a betting office.

Actually this practice is illegal as it contravenes the Gaming and Lotteries Acts, and if groups are caught gambling in this way they will be prosecuted, as was a group in Yorkshire! They had hired a hall and all the necessary equipment and the party was a great success. The idea appealed to members of the public who were charged £2 admission plus 50p per unit gambled on the horses. Betting was offered at various odds, and people were enjoying themselves. Unfortunately, the police were informed about the venture and they arrived in the middle of the proceedings and stopped a race. All those who had placed bets were forced to give their names and addresses, and the organisers were marched down to the police station to be charged. All the players were refunded entry fees, as they were denied the activity for which they had paid, and they found themselves unable to watch any more races. The organisers were each fined £100 in court for the offence, and though they were each given a conditional discharge rather than imprisonment it was a humiliating experience for all concerned. The group lost money instead of making it for their cause.

Horse racing games are very complex with regard to the law, and they are subjected to close scrutiny by the police and by officials from the Gaming and Lotteries Board. The *actual* racing of dogs and horses must be done on licensed tracks, and videos of races should only be shown on licensed premises.

Before embarking on a project like this, it is best to consult your chief of police. Give him all the details of your event, telling him the date, time and place of the race, and advise him which charity you are hoping to benefit. If he gives you permission to operate in his locality, then you are in luck. There are many variations of horse and dog racing, and you may find a loop-hole if you ask for professional help.

There are a few organisations that can legally supply your charity with a full evening's entertainment, based on filmed races. These companies often arrange to supply an operator too. All the 'betting' is done in such a way that the law is not contravened and the punters still have an exciting and profitable time, with quite a bit of money being made for the host organisers. It pays to look carefully at the offers in the papers and take advice and precautions. You cannot afford to fall foul of the law.

Part 3

GAMES SUITABLE FOR CLUBS, PUBS, FETES AND FAIRS

The games and competitions that follow can be used for either indoor or outdoor events. They have all proved popular money spinners, and they should bring fun and entertainment to fund-raising ventures.

Note: Throughout these games, there are prices suggested for 'having a go' and values suggested for prizes. Of course, these figures are easily changed according to the way your organisation sees its worth or assesses the spending potential of the punters. Clearly, if the fete or fair is being run mainly for participation by children, then high entry fees for the games are a definite no-no. As with all aspects of fund-raising, check your facts and plan ahead.

1 – The four card trick

Equipment needed
- Pack of cards

This competition is suitable for fetes or fairs.

Ask the friends and relatives of each member of your group to contribute a prize to the value of £2 or more, and approach local traders to contribute prizes to the value of £5 or more.

Set up your stall with shelves displaying the prizes. All the prizes valued at £2 or so should be on the lower shelves and prizes valued over £5 the higher shelves.

How to play
On a table in front of the prizes place five playing cards of any one suit, e.g. 2, 4, 6, 8 and 10 of hearts, diamonds, spades or clubs. The cards should be positioned so that the missing cards in the sequence can be put in the vacant places (i.e. so that, for example, the 3♣ can be put in between the 2♣ and the 4♣, and so on).

Contestants are offered two chances, as follows:

1. From the shuffled pack of cards in your hand, they can pay 20p to try to draw a card to fill one of the vacant places. If they draw a 3, 5, 7 or 9 of the right suit they win a small prize from the lower shelves.

2. For 30p they can make two draws from the shuffled pack to try to fill two of the vacant places. If they draw two of the missing cards, 3, 5, 7 or 9, they can take a prize from the top shelves. If they pick one only of the missing sequence they can choose a prize from the bottom shelves.

After each game, the cards are returned to the pack and reshuffled.

2 – Five penny guess

Equipment needed
- A large supply of 5p pieces.
- Ruled sheets to record the guesses.

How to play
Players are asked to guess how many pennies each person will choose to hold in their hands from a total of ten coins given to each player.

At the word 'go', all players, standing in a semicircle, will select a number of coins from none to ten to hold in their left hand. They hold the closed hand containing the coins in front of them. Each person will then guess the total amount of coins being held out of view. The guesses are recorded against the name of each player. Each guess will cost 20p.

The players then open their hands and the number of coins are counted. The person who guesses the number of coins correctly wins the prize. If more than one person chooses the right number of coins, then the names are put into a box and the winning name drawn by someone not playing the game.

You can ask members of the public how many coins will be held by a team of 25 players on a specified date. This gives your helpers a chance to sell guesses for, say, fourteen days prior to the event, and a lot more income will be raised.

A pub landlord may donate a prize because it brings extra people into his pub on the night, and publicity for the event is bound to be good for his business.

After the competition, when the winner has been selected, the game can be played over and over again, using the same coins. Players still pay 20p for each game that is played.

If the competition proves successful in your area, you could make it a regular Saturday evening event. It is a popular game and a real money spinner, yet very inexpensive to run.

3 – Split a thread

Equipment needed

- a self-standing unit designed to hold a bottle of whisky (see figure 3)
- bottles of whisky
- three darts
- button thread
- a thick piece of foam to catch the bottle

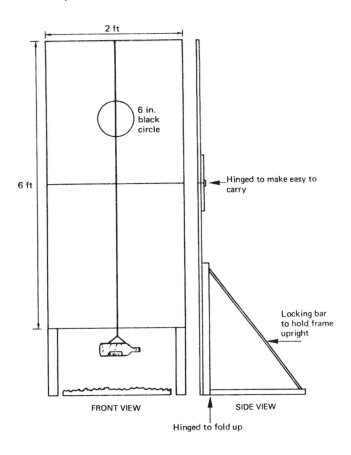

Figure 3 – Split a thread board

How to play

For a fee of 20p, a player is given three darts which he or she throws to try to split and break the thread that holds the bottle of whisky. If the thread is broken, the bottle will fall onto its foam rubber bed, and the player wins the whisky as his prize.

The throwing distance is the same as for competition darts.

The competition must be seen to be fair by all who play. If the thread is damaged in any way, it is replaced with a new length of thread.

It may be possible to obtain the bottle of whisky by sponsorship in return for naming the event after the brand (e.g. 'The TEACHERS Split-a-Thread').

How to make the apparatus

You need a length of chipboard, 6 ft x 2 ft. This is hung in position on a wooden frame so that the bottom of the board is 2 ft 6 in. from the ground. To make transport easier, you can use two pieces of chipboard, each 3 ft x 2 ft and hinged in the middle.

Paint a black circle, 6 in. in diameter on the chipboard, to show the button thread clearly. The circle should be in the centre of the board and 4 ft x 6 ins. from the ground.

The bottle is held in position by a length of button thread which is tied to a secure pin in the centre of the apparatus (see Figure 3). It is important that the thread is held tight against the board to enable the dart to sever it, and it should run down the middle of the circle.

4 – Chip ball

Equipment needed

- a piece of chipboard, 4 ft x 4 ft, mounted on timber edging 4 in. x 3/4 in
- cut five holes in the sheet of chipboard, each 2I/2 in. in diameter, in the positions shown in Figure 4
- place a washed empty baked bean tin into each hole; number each hole as shown
- golf club
- a supply of golf balls and tees.

How to play

From a starting point 6 ft away from the board, players have to try to chip a golf ball from a tee and into the tin to score 50 points or more to win a prize. Each player is given four golf balls, a tee and a golf club.

This popular game provides a great challenge; it can be a good money spinner and is suitable for any outdoor event.

Prizes should have a value of about £2 and players pay 20p for each game. As a special bonus you could offer a big prize for the highest score achieved at a fete. To do this you write down the scores of all those who score a total of 40 and over.

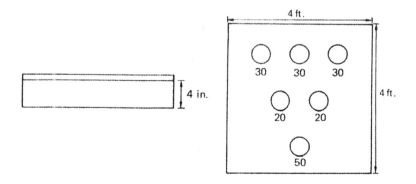

Figure 4 – Chipball

5 – The colour number game

Equipment needed

- a piece of hardboard, 2 ft square, marked off into 24 numbered squares, coloured as shown below
- three dice
- one dice, not numbered, but each side painted a different colour
- a plastic beaker
- a trestle table
- prizes valued from 75p to £3 (at least half should be valued over £1).

How to play

Paint the squares on the board in the following colours:

5 squares in white: Number the squares 12 17 21 24 and 6

5 squares in blue: Number the squares 4 10 16 20 and 22

3 squares in red: Number the squares 8 11 and 18

3 squares in yellow: Number the squares 7 9 and 15

4 squares in green: Number the squares 5 13 19 and 23

4 squares in orange: Number the squares 14 21 11 and 9

Contestants pay 20p for the chance to throw the four dice on the table from the plastic beaker. The three numbers on display are then added together, and if that number, together with the colour shown on the fourth dice, match the number of the same coloured square on the board, then the player wins a prize. Prizes should be listed according to the score achieved.

6 – The paper dart game

Equipment needed

- 1 piece of hardboard, 6 ft x 4 ft
- sufficient timber to make a stout frame for the board
- a trestle table
- paper darts.

How to make the equipment

Cut five 6 in. holes in the hardboard, in the positions illustrated in Figure 5, and number each hole with a score as shown.

The sheet of hardboard is held in position firmly by a wooden frame and mounted on supports.

Make at least 24 paper darts with stiff paper.

The board on its frame should be placed at a distance of 4 ft from a trestle table. Place the darts in groups of four on the table.

How to play

The public pay 20p to try to glide the four darts through the holes on the board.

The appearance of the board is improved if you know of an artist who will paint comic faces, using the holes as mouths. If painted in bright colours, it attracts people to the stall and makes the game more fun for spectators to watch.

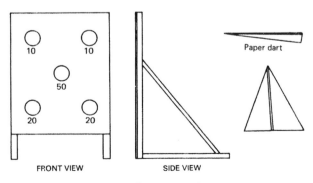

Figure 5 – The paper dart game

7 – Guess the order in which six cards will be drawn

Equipment needed
- one pack of playing cards
- one sweet jar, painted a bright colour
- prepared chart on which to record the guesses.

How to play
The object of the game is to guess which six cards will be drawn from a jar containing a pack of playing cards. The order in which each card is to be drawn is recorded on a prepared chart (see Figure 6). The cards can all be drawn by one member of the public, or each card can be drawn by six individuals.

This game can be made into a big event by inviting people from six different pubs to participate in the game. The draw is made in one pub and the results are then phoned through to all the other pubs participating.

It is also possible to keep playing this game each night for a week, recording guesses in each pub each night. If preferred, one card only can be drawn from each of six pubs on one specified night of the week.

The game is also successful in shopping centres and at fetes, when people are asked to guess the order of cards to be drawn that day. It is very hard to guess the actual cards drawn, and if no one guesses correctly, the game can extend over a number of weeks until someone is successful.

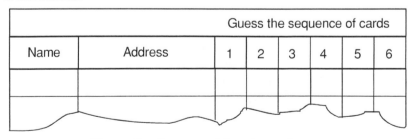

Name	Address	Guess the sequence of cards					
		1	2	3	4	5	6

Figure 6 – Score card for six card game

8 – 'Pick the pairs' card game

Equipment needed
- a lot of small prizes valued from £1 to £5
- a trestle table and three shelves to hold the prizes
- a pack of playing cards.

How to play
The game organiser sets out 52 playing cards face down on a table and invites people to pay 20p for a chance to pick out two matching cards, i.e. two kings or two queens.

If two aces are selected, then the winner can choose a prize from the shelf which contains the top prizes to the value of about £5.

Kings, queens and jacks give a prize from the second shelf (mid-value prizes). Two of any cards of the same number, from two to ten, give a low-value prize from the bottom shelf.

Provided that you display the rules clearly, you could exclude some pairs, say fives, tens and kings, from the winning sets.

If possible, get the prizes donated by local shopkeepers, because then the overheads will be nil and all your takings will be profit.

After each game the cards must be reshuffled so that each player has an even chance of winning and cannot benefit from remembering the previous position of cards.

9 – Guess the contents of five tins

Equipment needed
- five tins of foodstuffs, each to be clearly numbered from 1 to 5
- record the contents of each tin, together with the number of the tin, and keep this information in a sealed envelope
- steam the labels off the tins
- prepared chart to record entries

How to play
People pay an entry fee to try to guess the contents of each tin. Details of each player's name and address and the guess at the contents of each numbered tin must be recorded. At the end of the competition, the tins are opened in public to reveal their contents. Alternatively, each player could complete a simple entry form and hand it in with the fee.

The winner is the person who has guessed the contents of each tin correctly. If there is no winner, select the person who has guessed all the contents but who has given the wrong numbers. If there is still no winner, then the person with the most correct guesses wins the prize. You may be able to persuade a food manufacturer to donate money to buy a good prize. Alternatively, offer a hamper of goodies valued around £50 and persuade friends to donate a contribution to the hamper. Make out a list of what you would like, and cross off the list every item that is received.

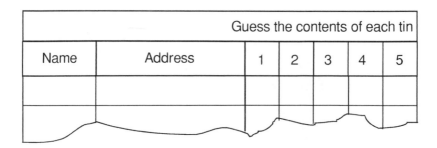

Name	Address	Guess the contents of each tin				
		1	2	3	4	5

Figure 7 – Sample entry form

10 – The bottle and coin game

Equipment needed
- a bottle of gin or other spirits
- sheet of hardboard, 3 ft square
- bottle and chalk.

This game can be played at dances, in pub lounges, and at indoor and outdoor fetes, and is usually very popular. There are no expenses involved if you can get someone to donate the prize.

How to play
Place the hardboard on the ground, and put your bottle in the centre. Around the base of the bottle draw a circle which is the width of the base of the bottle plus three times the diameter of a 10p piece. As seen from Figure 8, this leaves a space around the base of the bottle of 11/2 times the width of a 10p piece.

People are invited to throw their 10p pieces at the bottle from a distance of 6 ft away, in an endeavour to get the coin to rest inside the circle without touching the ring.

All successful entries have their name and address recorded and placed in a box. The winner of the bottle of spirits will be the person whose name is drawn.

Every coin thrown is donated to your cause.

If no one succeeds in landing a coin successfully, then the game survives to be played at another venue at a later date.

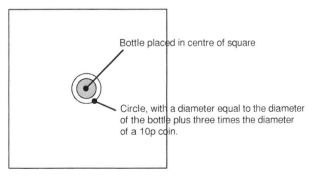

Figure 8 – The bottle and coin game

11 – How many pennies will it take to enclose a circle?

Equipment needed
- a large piece of hardboard or chipboard
- a length of string, a large plain pin and a black felt-tip pen
- prepared charts to record guesses.

This is a very simple competition to operate at an indoor or outdoor event.

How to play
Fix a length of string to the centre of the hardboard with a pin. Tie the felt-tip at the other end and carefully draw a large circle, 3 or 4 feet in diameter.. Display the circle out of reach of competitors so that they cannot measure its circumference.

People pay a fee of 20p to guess the number of pennies it will take to enclose the circle you have drawn. Record the guesses on a prepared chart. The winner is the person who guesses nearest to the correct number of pennies needed.

At the end of the event, measure the number, using a penny coin, marking it off as you enclose the circle (see Figure 9).

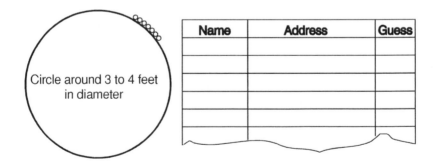

Figure 9 – Pennies in a circle

12 – How many 10p pieces to reach a certain height

How to play

Choose an object at your fete that you want to be the target, and ask players to guess how many 10p pieces you would have to stack on top of one another to reach the height of the object. It could be an entrance door, the height of the hall, or the height of two people when one person is standing on the shoulders of the other! You can even make a scaffold type frame for this event, but it is obviously important to choose a height that cannot easily be measured.

Charge 20p for each guess, and record the guesses on a prepared chart, as used in Figure 9. (As with several of the games where you need to record entries, produce a simple chart on a computer (ask someone to do it for you if you do not have access to one) and run off several copies – this will save you some of the work!)

At the end of the competition, measure the object you have chosen, to its full height, and divide this figure by the thickness of a 10p piece (1/16 in). The nearest to the correct guess wins the prize.

13 – Ring a circle

Equipment needed
- one sheet of hardboard, 3 ft square
- five screw tops from soft drinks bottles.

How to play

Draw a series of circles all over the hardboard. The circles should vary in size from 1 in. to 3 in. diameter. Number the circles with scores 5 up to 25, with the larger circle getting the lower scores. For an entry fee of 20p, each player is given five bottle tops which he must throw from a line four feet away. The aim is to land the bottle top inside one of the circles without touching the edges of the circle.

People must get a score of 25 or more to win a prize.

14 – Score nudge ball

Equipment needed

- six sponge type tennis balls, each dyed a different colour
- one ordinary tennis ball
- a sheet of hardboard, 4 ft square.

How to play

Into the hardboard cut six holes of 2 in. diameter. These holes should be positioned in a straight row, about 1 in. above the base of the hardboard (see Figure 10). Paint a coloured circle around each hole, to match each coloured ball. The game is then built into a frame to raise it from the ground and the balls are placed in a horizontal row, 9 in. in front of the hole of the same colour.

People pay 20p to throw the ordinary tennis ball at each of the coloured balls in turn in an attempt to nudge them into holes of the same colour from a distance of 6 ft away. If players get all six balls into the appropriate holes they win a prize valued around £3-4. If they manage only four or five they win a prize valued at £1.

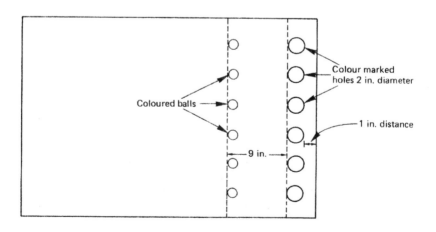

Figure 10 – Score nudge ball.

15 – The bottle tops contest

Equipment needed
- a sheet of hardboard, 3 ft square, with a piece of 1/2 in dowel stuck into the centre (see Figure 11)
- a supply of metal tops from soft drink bottles
- a measuring tape.

How to play
Draw circles around the dowel, each a 1/2 in. greater than the previous circle, until you have drawn 10.

Players are given five bottle tops which they have to toss from a throwing line nine feet from the centre of the dowel in an attempt to get them as close to the dowel as possible. Tops that land with the cork side up or on the edges of circles are out.

If a bottle top is touching the dowel when it comes to rest, the player scores 10 points. There is an extra score of 2 points for every top that lands the right way up within a circle (if it is not touching the circumference). If a bottle top hits another top off its target, the points for that top are lost. If the bottle top knocks another top clear of a line, then an extra 2 points are gained.

There is a small prize for those who score 10 points or more. This event can be run as a team contest, with four members to a team. In this case it is the team with the highest number of points that wins the contest.

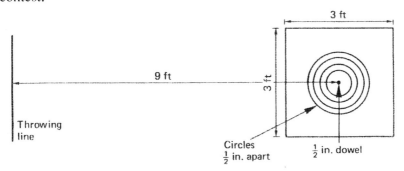

Figure 11 – The bottle tops contest

16 – Land in the circle

Equipment needed
- three plastic buckets

How to play
This is a fascinating game to play, either at an indoor event or out of doors, and all you need is three plastic buckets. In the centre of each paint a circle which is 11/2 times the diameter of a 10p coin. Now fill the bucket with water, up to 2 in. from the rim.

Invite people to drop their 10p coins into the bucket, from the height of the bucket handle, in an attempt to land the coin in the centre of the circle.

Coins that land outside the circle, or which touch the circumference line, are forfeited. People who land their coin inside the circle, without touching the edge, win the return of their coin plus a small prize.

Remove the coins from the bucket frequently, as they can prove an obstacle for other players.

17 – Nod the ball

Equipment needed
- an 8 ft x 4 ft piece of chipboard
- wooden supports
- three buckets
- three medium-sized footballs
- a trestle table.

How to play
Fix the three buckets at different levels on an upright board (see Figure 13). Put the balls on a table 6 ft away from the board.

The player heads the balls, one at a time, to try to aim them into the bucket from his side of the table.

If the player manages to aim all three balls into a bucket, he wins a prize valued at about £3-4. If he aims two balls into buckets, then he wins a prize of about £1.

You should have a selection of small prizes on show. Teddy bears can be purchased very cheaply in bulk, and they are popular prizes to use for this competition, which tends to attract young people.

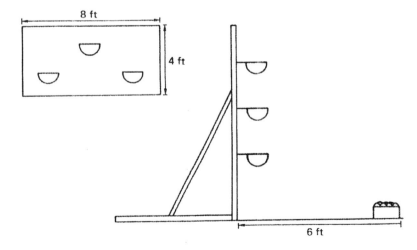

8 ft

4 ft

6 ft

Figure 12 – Nod the ball

97

18 – Lucky dart prize

Equipment needed
- a length of chipboard, 6 ft x 4 ft, held upright by supporting brackets (see Figure 13)
- four wooden boxes, 4 in deep, 6 in Long and 4 in wide, built onto the chipboard
- button thread which runs through the centre of 6 in black circles
- four darts.

How to play

Four black circles are painted on the chipboard, equal distances apart (as shown in Figure 13). A length of button thread is pinned above each circle, and the bottom of the thread is tied to the lid of each wooden box.

Each contestant pays 25p for a chance to throw four darts. The aim is to sever the thread to open the box and reveal a prize hidden inside. Darts must be thrown from a line 8 ft away for the men and 7 ft away for women. The prizes could be shopping vouchers or small wrapped objects that will fit into the boxes.

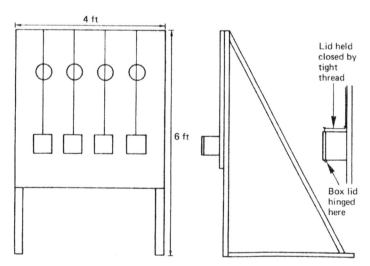

Figure 13 – Lucky darts

19 – Matching scores

Equipment needed
- one dartboard
- three darts
- 180 discs numbered from 1 to 150 (placed number side down on the table).

How to play
Contestants pay 20p for the chance to throw three darts.

The score of the three darts is added together, and the total number is recorded. The player is then invited to pick up a disc. If the number on the underside of the disc is the same as the total score number achieved, he wins a prize.

20 – Score a prize

Equipment needed
- one dartboard
- three darts
- discs numbered from 1 to 180
- small sticky labels on which the word PRIZE is printed. Plus extra labels.

How to play
The 150 discs lie face upwards on a table and players throw three darts at the board. If the players scores a total of 36, he is invited to pick up the disc showing the same number to see if he has won a prize. If there is a sticky PRIZE label under the disc, the player can pick any prize on display.

The player's disc is returned to the table, minus its label. Another labelled disc must then be added, but do not let anyone see its number.

21 – The shuffle spot game

Equipment needed
- 36 blocks of wood, 1 in. square, 1/2 in. deep
- one tray.

How to play
Paint the blocks of wood blue on all six sides. On four blocks, paint a small white circle on one square side only; on another four blocks, paint a small red circle.

All the wooden blocks are placed on a tray with the painted circles hidden from view.

People pay 20p for a chance to try to turn nine blocks in the hope of finding four circles of one colour.

After each attempt, the blocks should be well shuffled so that onlookers cannot benefit from watching where the blocks with circles are placed. It may be safer to cover the blocks with a cloth while shuffling.

A prize valued at about £2 is suitable.

22 – Roller disc

Equipment needed

- four discs for each person. These should be 3 in. in diameter and they are made from hardboard
- one roller disc board, made as follows: One sheet of hardboard, 6 ft x 4 ft, with four channel ways, 30 in Long, 1¼ in wide and 1/2 in deep (see Figure 14)
- at the end of each channel, a hole 3½ in in diameter.

How to play

The object of the game is to roll the disc along the board in an attempt to get it into the channel way that will take it into a hole to score 10. This game is not as easy as it looks because the discs need power of movement to take them to the score holes. Only discs that drop into the holes are counted.

Each player is given four discs to roll. There is a prize for those who score 30 or more, with a fee of 20p for each game, and prizes should be valued at around £3.

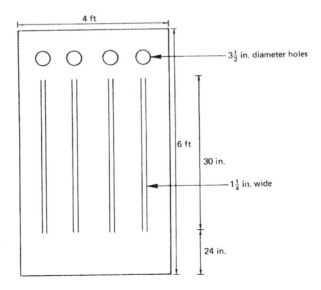

Figure 14 – The roller disc board

23 – The dice score competition

Equipment needed
- ten dice, all numbered 1 to 6
- one long glass tumbler.

How to play
Players are asked to roll the dice from the tumbler to see what score they can achieve. The highest score of the day is the winner.

After each game, the name and address of the player and the score achieved is written down on a prepared chart. As soon as a new record score is achieved, this figure is displayed to encourage other people to try to beat the score.

It is a good idea to have at least three prizes for those who have scored the highest by the end of the day.

Charge a fee of 20p for each game.

24 – Dart score 20-50

Equipment needed
- one dartboard
- three darts
- plastic straws containing strips of paper, some bearing the word 'prize',

How to play
Players are given three darts and a chance to try to score between 20 and 50 on the board. If they score within these figures, they pick a straw containing a small slip of paper which will either be blank or have the word PRIZE printed across it.

Some of the prizes should be very attractive to encourage people to play the game. Other smaller prizes can be valued at £1 or so.

If the player scores 50 or more with the third dart, he can take two straws instead of one.

25 – Match your score

Equipment needed
- one dartboard
- three darts
- 100 numbered discs.

How to play
Discs are placed face down on the table and for 20p a player can pick up a disc to reveal a number from 1 to 100.

The player is then asked to try to score the number he has selected by throwing his darts to the same number on the dartboard. He wins a prize if he can score this number with either one dart or all three darts!

26. – Throw a straw

Equipment needed
- two large boxes of plastic straws
- three round goldfish bowls
- table.

How to play
The equipment needed for this game is cheap and easy to obtain and yet it has appeal, especially for children.

Place the three goldfish bowls in the shape of a triangle on a table. The table should be placed about 4 ft from the throwing line.

People pay 15p for six full-length straws, and they try to aim them, one at a time, into the goldfish bowls. If they get one straw into each of the three bowls, they win a prize valued around £1. Any player who gets extra straws into a goldfish bowl wins a small additional prize.

27 – The hat stand game

Equipment needed
- a hat stand; maybe you can borrow one from a friend, or alternatively you may find one in a junk shop
- a selection of hats – straw hats, soft hats, hard hats, and any hat for man or woman that you can borrow for the day.

How to play
Players pay 20p to choose four hats in an attempt to throw two of them onto the hat stand from a distance of 6 ft away. If they throw more than two hats onto the stand, and they hang properly, the player has a bonus prize.

People love to choose funny hats to throw, and this game gives a lot of amusement to players. They often choose the hard hats thinking that they will be easier to throw, when actually they tend to bounce back and do not settle easily on a hat stand.

28 – The cup and saucer game

Equipment needed
- nine plastic cups
- nine plastic saucers
- five table tennis balls
- a table.

How to play
The cups and saucers are stacked in threes, one on top of another, as in Figure 15, and placed on a table which is 6 ft away from the throwing line.

Players pay 20p for five table tennis balls. They have to get two balls into one cup, without knocking the cup over. Successful players win prizes valued at about £1.50, which may have been donated by a sponsor.

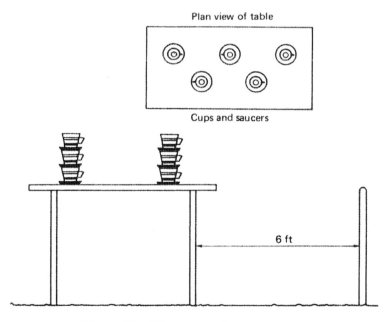

Figure 15 – The cup and saucer game

29 – The nuts and bolts game

Equipment needed

- 10 nuts and 10 bolts of slightly different sizes
- five extra nuts with no matching bolts
- one wooden board, 18 in square
- a stop watch.

How to play

When selecting the bolts, make sure that you select a group that appear to be almost the same thickness although they have a different thread pattern. Mix imperial and metric sizes too. Drill 15 appropriate sized holes through the wooden board so that you can fit the bolts tightly, to leave the open threaded ends exposed (see Figure 16).

Players are given 30 seconds to try to fit each nut on to the appropriate bolt. Each person who succeeds in completing the task in the time wins a modest prize.

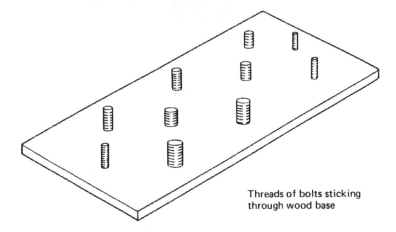

Threads of bolts sticking
through wood base

Figure 16 – The nuts and bolts game

30 – Guess the numbers present on the day

This competition requires the consent of your local pub landlord, but it is popular with the regulars, and fun to play, so this should not prove difficult!

How to play

The aim of the game is to guess how many people were present in a pub bar on four specific dates during the previous month.

The landlord counts his customers each day, and records the total number on a slip of paper that he inserts in an envelope and seals. This envelope is left on display at the bar until the end of the competition. There is a fee of 20p to guess the number of people in the pub on the four specified evenings. Guesses are recorded on prepared charts (see Figure 17). The player is given a numbered cloakroom ticket, and the number of the ticket, its colour and the player's name and address and four guesses are recorded for easy reference. When a player knows he has made the correct guesses, he just tells the organiser his ticket number and his answers can be speedily checked.

At the end of the competition, a member of the public is invited to open the sealed envelope and read out the results. If there is no completely correct answer, then the nearest to correct guesses of a player will win the prize. This game brings extra customers into the pub and you may be able to persuade a brewery to sponsor the prize.

Ticket no	Colour	Name	Address	day 1	day 2	day 3	day 4

Figure 17 – Guess the numbers present

31 – Spin your name to win a prize

Equipment needed
- timber support, with a sturdy blockboard base
- plywood disc 3 ft diameter.

How to play
You need to build an upright stand, as show in Figure 18. Print the letters of the alphabet at random, three times around the circumference of the disc. The disc is then mounted on the axle, as illustrated. It must be well balanced so that when it is spun it will not stop in the same position each time. The disc must turn freely. Fixed above the disc is an arrow with a sharp point to show quite clearly at which letter the arrow is pointing.

Contestants pay 20p for a chance to spin the disc and spell their own names. First they write their first names on a sheet of paper; then they are given twice as many spins as there are letters in the name, and they attempt to spin all the letters that make up their first names. Each letter that stops by the arrow is written down.

Those who succeed in spinning the letters needed can select a prize. Aim to get prizes valued at around £2.

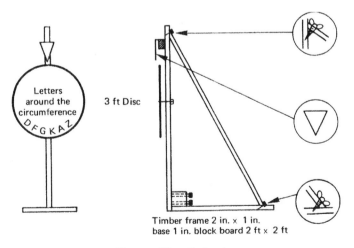

Figure 18 – Spin the name

32 – Guess the height of the marks on car wheels

Each tyre on a car is marked with an arrow in surveyor's chalk and people are asked to guess, to the nearest tenth of an inch, the height that the point of the arrow on each tyre will be above the ground after the car has travelled 200 yards. The marks on the tyres should be at the edge of the tread as illustrated in Figure 19.

The person who guesses nearest to the correct heights on each of the four wheels wins the prize.

To enable the organiser to spot the winner quickly, it is best to record all the entries on prepared charts so that they can see at a glance who has made correct guesses. If there is more than one winner the names are put into a box and the winning entry is drawn. With a view to obtaining sponsorship, you could ask a car manufacturer or showroom to provide a car, suitably adorned with its own advertising, for the competition. They may be willing to offer a good prize for this unique way of advertising their car.

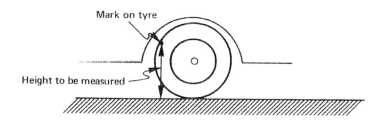

Figure 19 – The marks on car wheels

ENTRY FORM

GUESS THE HEIGHT OF THE TYRE MARKS COMPETITION

You are asked to guess the height from the ground that the mark on each of the four wheels of the car will be after the car has travelled a distance of 200 yards.

Wheel 1. Near-side front .... Wheel 2. Near-side rear ....

Wheel 3. Off-sidefront .... Wheel 4. Off-side rear ....

Name ....

Address ....

....

The judges decision is final and binding on all entries

Please detach and retain for your own reference.

Wheel 1.........
Wheel 2.........
Wheel 3.........
Wheel 4........

33 – The tyre mountain game

Equipment needed
- a good supply of 13 in tyres (or Mini tyres) – these can usually be borrowed from your local tyre depot
- one pole for each team, 7 ft high and 4 in. in diameter
- two heavy wooden beams for each pole about 4 ft long, 9 in wide and 4 in thick

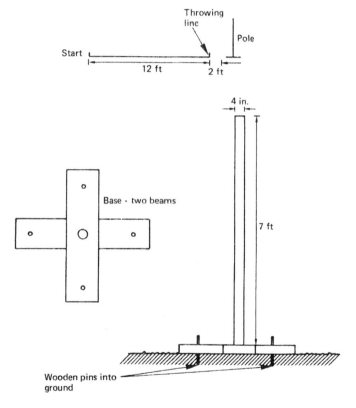

Figure 20 – The tyre mountain game

How to play
The object of the game is for teams of four people to compete to see how quickly they can roll the tyres up a course 12 ft long and then ring

the tyres over the top of a pole from a throwing line 2 ft from the base of the pole.

Only one member of the team is allowed to roll a tyre towards the pole at one time. The next team member must wait until he returns to the base line before starting off with his tyre. The team that rings the most tyres in three minutes wins the game.

This competition is suitable mainly for outdoor fetes because it requires soft ground in order to pin down the base of each pole (see Figure 20).   It should be possible to get a large number of teams to play if you ask pubs, clubs and local business organisations to take part; you could then run the game in heats of four at a time, with the winning team going forward to the next round. Aim to get as many teams as possible because this can be a very exciting event both for players and spectators.

Maybe the firm that lends you the tyres will also sponsor the prize.

34 – Balls in a ring

Equipment needed
- ten soft foam tennis balls, plain colour
- five red foam tennis balls
- one thin circular disc of plywood, 3 ft in diameter.

How to play
Ten plain coloured balls are placed on to the plywood 'ring' and the player is given five red balls which he can roll or toss to try to remove the plain balls from the disc from a distance of 10 ft.

The player wins 5 points for each plain ball that he rolls clear of the centre. For a higher score, he must try to make his coloured ball come to rest inside the 'ring'. If he succeeds in this, he gets 10 points for each plain ball that he rolls out of the circle.

A prize can be offered for any player who scores 30 points or more. A major prize could also be offered to the player with the highest score at the end of the day.

This game is very competitive when two or more people challenge each other. It is also a very successful team game, with groups of four people competing against each other. In this event you charge a fee for each team to enter the competition, and you can raise extra money by asking people to gamble on which team will win the prize. Charge for each guess.

35 – The water bottle game

Equipment needed
- hot-water bottles
- basket-ball stand with net (borrowed from a local school)
- stopwatch

How to play
The hot-water bottles should be half filled with water; do not fill them completely as this makes them easier to throw. With half-filled bottles, the water moves about inside, causing them to move in an irregular fashion through the air and this makes the competition more fun.

Each contestant is given 90 seconds to throw as many bottles as he or she can through the top of the net from a throwing distance of 6 ft away from the stand.

The highest score achieved should be written up on a display so that people know the top score that they have to beat. Charge 20p per game.

It is worth while writing to manufacturers of hot-water bottles to canvas their support. They may donate the bottles, or give money for prizes: £50.00 would enable you to buy a very attractive prize for the two highest scorers.

36 – Guess the items photographed

For this competition, you need a good photographer to take 10 quality colour prints of objects that have been photographed from an unusual angle. This fascinating game can be played on social occasions and at events where there is very little space for more active games.

Only the organiser must know which objects have been photographed, and they must be difficult to recognise from the angle the picture is taken. Each photograph is placed securely on a sheet of card and given a number, 1 to 10. Alternatively, they can be mounted on ten individual numbered cards.

People pay 20p to guess what items have been photographed. They record their guesses on an entry form, and at the end of the event the person who has the most correct answers wins the prize. If there is more than one correct entry, the winning slips are put into a drum and the winner's name drawn out in public.

An interesting variation of this game is to have the photographer picture things which can be found around the locality, but still from an unusual angle or in great close-up – such as pub signs, church roof gargoyles, unusual ornaments, street signs and so on. Of course, this does give a slight advantage to local people – it depends on the catchment area for your event.

Write the name of each object shown in the photographs

1_____ 2_____ 3_____ 4_____ 5_____

6_____ 7_____ 8_____ 9_____ 10_____

Name ....

Address ....

....

The judges' decision is final and binding on all contestants.

---

37 – Guess how long it takes for a pint of water to boil dry

Equipment needed
- a pint measure and water
- an old saucepan
- a calor gas stove (use whatever pressure you like to boil the water)
- a stopwatch.

How to play
The stopwatch is started as soon as the flame under the saucepan is lit, and people pay 20p to guess to the nearest tenth of a second the time it will take for the last drop of water to fizzle dry from the bottom of the container.

The nearest guess to the correct time is the winner. The name and address of each contestant should be recorded on a prepared chart, and the result announced as soon as the winner is known. If there is more than one correct guess, the entries should be placed in a box and the winning name drawn by a member of public.

38 – Guess the number of balloons to fill a greenhouse

Equipment needed
- a large supply of balloons of varying sizes, and an inflation system, preferably a gas bottle
- a greenhouse.

How to play
People pay 20p to guess how many balloons have been used to fill a greenhouse on display. The person who guesses nearest to the correct number of balloons is the winner.

All guesses are recorded on prepared charts. If your members sell entries to the competition away from the site of the greenhouse, they must have photographs and written details of its actual size and dimensions so that all competitors can make an educated guess. To complicate matters put a number of small balloons out of view in the middle.

The competition can be held in supermarkets and shopping precincts, or in a large hall. If the event is run in a shopping area, then operate on Fridays and Saturdays when there are many more shoppers. Approach greenhouse manufacturers or garden centres and ask them to donate a greenhouse as a prize. In return you will offer to exhibit the greenhouse in a prominent position and allow them to display their advertising material on the unit. The balloons attract a lot of attention to their product so you are offering a unique form of advertising and publicity.

If you need a trailer to move the greenhouse, ask for one from a transport firm in return for advertising.

39 – How high will the water rise?

Equipment needed
- a glass tank capable of holding **well over** the total quantity of water used **plus** the largest object in the game
- a sheet of paper or a tape measure, graduated in tenths of an inch or millimetres, stuck to the side of the glass container
- water, about a third of the way up the container
- items used to measure the displacement of water:
  1. a large chunk of rock
  2. a 56 lb weight
  3. one large potato
  4. three tins of peas.

How to play
People pay 20p to guess how many tenths of an inch the water will rise as each of the four separate items on the list is lowered into the

water. The measurement of the water level is taken before and after each item is added. Alternatively, you can ask for just one guess as all the items are lowered into the tank at one time.

Guesses are submitted on prepared entry forms or a master chart and the nearest to an all correct guess is the winner.

40 – Who can grow the tallest sunflower?

This is a popular competition for children who love to watch the sunflower as it grows to its full height from a seed. It is particularly good for schools and clubs because the children can be taught to plant their own sunflower seed in a suitable container (a margarine tub is ideal for the first few months of growth). A fee of 10p is charged for each sunflower seed.

Obviously the competition has to be planned well in advance of a special event, fete or fair, to give each child an opportunity to grow his own plant. All the seeds are planted on the same day, and children will exhibit their flowers on the day of the event, to find which has grown the tallest. The winner gets a prize of about £10. If there are other competitions to be held at the same time as the judging of the height of sunflowers, the group can make extra money by charging an entry fee to the event.

Children are very proud of their sunflowers, and they love to see them on exhibition. They like the challenge of growing a taller plant than anyone else.

41 – Guess the weight of the dog

This can be a real winner if you can beg the loan of a friendly, well groomed dog that enjoys all the attention it receives.

To weigh the dog, you first weigh someone on his own, and then with the dog in his arms; the difference is the weight of the dog, which is written down and stored in a sealed envelope.

How to play

People are charged a fee of 20p to guess the weight of the dog. Each guess is recorded together with the name and address of the contestant.

The dog will attract the crowds to his stand by his friendliness, making this a popular competition.

42 – Guess the age of the cat

This is a popular game if you can find a placid and friendly cat that will not mind attention from children! If possible, borrow a wire cat box so that the cat can easily be seen, and make it a comfortable bed to lie on.

People pay 20p to guess the age of the cat, and their names and guesses are recorded on a prepared chart. The winner is the person who guesses the correct age by the end of the fete. If more than one person makes a correct guess, put the names into a box and draw out the winner.

Part 4

COMPETITIONS WITH TEAMS AND PEOPLE COMPETING AGAINST EACH OTHER

43 – Children's tin can obstacle race

Equipment needed for one obstacle course (five recommended)

- a large number of empty baked bean tins (drill two holes in the bottom and put a length of string through the holes)
- five armbands, each of a different colour
- two planks
- two wooden blocks to support each plank
- six traffic cones to each player
- two lengths of thick chipboard, approx. 4 ft long
- tickets in five different colours (stamped with the race number prior to each race)
- a supply of cards in each of the five different colours
- a stamp to record the number of each race.

How to play

This is an exciting game for children, who like the challenge of walking on empty tins, and of course spectators enjoy watching their efforts.

Children pay 25p to enter a race, which is run in heats of five players. Each child is given a coloured arm band, and spectators are asked to bet 10p on the winner of each race. Those who place bets are given a card of the colour they choose to win, and this is stamped with the race number prior to each heat.

Each child is given two empty tins which they step onto as if they were stilts. They are held in place by the lengths of string held in each hand (see Figure 22).

Contestants are asked to race across a course of about 50 yards and to negotiate the following three obstacles on route:

1. After five yards, they climb over two planks raised about ten inches from the ground by wooden blocks.

2. Ten yards further they negotiate the traffic cones.

3. After a further ten yards, they make their way up a sloping sheet of chipboard which is raised by a wooden block at one end. Then they walk down a second length of chipboard to the ground and race to the finishing line.

121

If you organise this game in several heats, a book token or other prize valued at about £10 would be suitable, with prizes of a lesser value for those who come second and third in the race.

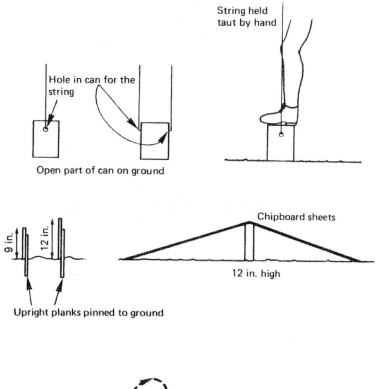

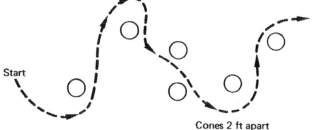

Figure 22 – Children's tin-can obstacle race

44 – Target putting

Equipment needed
- a circular target score mat, in plastic or Velcro (see Figure 23)
- an indoor bowling green if the event is to be held indoors (you may be able to borrow a green from a manufacturer).

How to play
The target is placed 25 ft from the drive-off position on the green, and each golfer is allowed five golf balls which he will try to putt into the circle that gives the highest score. This competition can be run as a team event, with four golfers to each team. The player with the highest score in each team goes into the next round. It is also popular when run on a larger scale with several teams competing for the highest score in about six different venues. In this case, the winners from each team meet at a special sporting event to compete in the finals. If the event was held twice weekly in each of six halls, the competition should be completed within four weeks. For a big competition like this the entry fee could be £5 and you should try to encourage up to 5,000 golfers to take part. Send entry forms to all golf clubs within a radius of thirty miles.

A good prize would be a complete set of golf clubs and accessories plus a trophy for which players could compete on an annual basis.

Spectators pay 50p to watch the competition as friends and relatives of the players usually enjoy the fun.

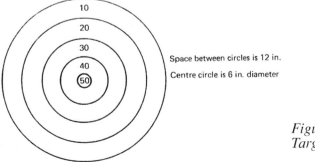

Space between circles is 12 in.

Centre circle is 6 in. diameter

Figure 23 –
Target putting

45 – Guess the time it takes to play nine holes of golf

People are asked to guess to the nearest minute how long it will take two golfers to play nine holes of golf. Timing starts from the moment the first ball is driven off at the first tee, and is stopped when the last ball is holed at the ninth green.

Golfers enjoy this competition because it taxes their ability to forecast something in connection with their own sporting hobby. Again, try the manufacturers of golf equipment for sponsorship. You could provide advertising in the form of boards carried by members of the group whilst the game is in progress. You could also offer to call the competition after the company name or product in return for sponsorship.

Players should be advised of the event well in advance of the date of the competition. There should be a notice about the event on the club notice board, giving date, time and place to attend. People then sign their names if they agree to take part in the competition and pay their entry fee in advance of the event.

46 – Golf driving bonanza

Equipment needed
- 100 golf balls
- a reliable stop watch.

How to play
Contestants are asked to guess to the nearest second how long it will take two local golfers to drive 100 golf balls from a tee on the golf course. The golfers take it in turn to drive off.

The condition of the golf balls in unimportant, so try to collect old balls from friendly golfers! Alternatively you could ask a golf ball manufacturer to donate the golf balls, and these could be auctioned after the event to add extra money to your funds. You may be able to borrow a stop watch from the sports master at your local school.

47 – The three golf ball challenge

For this competition you need the cooperation of your local golf club and its professional.

How to play

You invite contestants to guess, to the nearest inch, the total distance that the golfing professional (or any other recognisable personality who is a good golfer) will drive three golf balls from one particular tee on the course. The first ball might travel, say, 106 yd, 1 ft, 3 in.; the second 98 yd, 1 ft, 2 in.; and the third 92 yd, 6½ in. This makes the total distance for the three drives 296 yd, 2 ft, 11 in. The contestant who guesses nearest to this figure wins the prize.

This competition can be a lot of fun. There are many factors governing the results on the day which cannot be known in advance – for instance, whether the ground is wet or dry and whether there is wind or rain – and the golfing fraternity will usually support the event for this reason.

Any form of golfing equipment, preferably donated by a manufacturer or retail outlet, would be suitable for a prize. Make sure that the date, time and place of the event are well advertised.

Note that measuring the distance of each drive will present some difficulty, as you need to be accurate to the inch. One option is to obtain a very large ball of stout twine and, before the event, mark it at, say, 10 yard intervals between 150 and 250 yards and use a surveyor's measure for the final short distance between your mark and the ball. Alternatively, you could set up markers on the fairway or on a driving range and measure from them. Either way, you will need to be as accurate as possible, to avoid disputes.

48 – Inter-school cycle polo

PTAs and youth clubs could raise a few pounds with this venture as there is no capital outlay involved.

Equipment needed
- each child uses his or her own cycle and a polo stick (which can be made in the school workshops)
- a playing field.

How to play
This is a fast game, and the rules are the same as the rules for polo played on ponies. It is a popular event for children who own bicycles, and it can very successfully be organised as a major inter-school competition, when a charge of £5 is made for each school team entering the game.

Sports goods manufacturers are good sponsors for such events because the game draws the name of their products to the attention of children who will be their customers of the future.

49 – Radio-controlled car racing

This is a popular game for young people, and parent teacher groups will find it a good way of raising funds if they organise the event on a league basis, covering all schools within a certain area.

Model clubs are often pleased to assist in this sort of venture if they are approached in the right way. They like to draw attention to the existence of the club and open the door to possible new recruits. Ask the club to lend you their model cars and track for the event. Model car owners can often be persuaded to support a particular school, and may undertake to teach one or more pupils how to operate and race their cars.

How to play
Each team should be asked to pay £5 to enter a team in the league, and

the PTA will compile a fixture list of events.

The school gymnasium or canteen is usually the best venue for this event as it is possible to put a large number of seats around the area for spectators. You should aim to cater for about 150 people including spectators and players.

Each school retains the proceeds of entry fees from the spectators and the takings can add a handsome profit to the cause.

50 – The newspaper relay race

Equipment needed
- approx. 500 newspapers for each team (the papers must all be the same size and shape, so, if possible, enlist the support of a local newspaper)
- three shoulder bags for each team (suitable for carrying newspapers)
- five stopwatches for each team
- one trestle table for each team.

How to play
Find at least six teams of six members each with one helper for each member of the team.

The route of the relay race should be down town or village streets where spectators can watch the fun. The distance should be within a radius of about six miles, with the start and finish of the race being at the same place. Members of the teams are placed equal distances apart on the route, together with a helper to supervise activities and to check the times.

The aim of the game is to transport as many newspapers as possible from one point to the next in the shortest time, scoring as follows: a team is credited with 1 point for every newspaper carried, and the first runners are given 10 seconds to fill their shoulder bags with as many newspapers as they can. The more papers carried, the higher the score at the finish. The first runners then follow the route for 1 mile until they reach the change-over point where the next member of the team is waiting. The first runners are then given 10 seconds to fill a second shoulder bag with as many newspapers as they can. When time is called the second runner takes the two bags and continues running for a further mile on the route.

On reaching the next checkpoint, the second runners will be given 10 seconds to fill a third bag with as many newspapers as possible, and the third runners continue the journey with all three bags but they run for only half a mile.

The fourth, fifth and sixth runners do not have to add any extra newspapers. They just take the three bags and continue with the next half mile of the race.

The time of the last runner to reach the finish in each team is recorded in minutes and seconds. He or she is then given 20 seconds to stack onto the table all the newspapers carried in the three bags.

To score points for the team, each newspaper represents 1 second of time. At the end of the 20 seconds, the number of stacked newspapers is counted and subtracted from the time it took to run the race for example 72 newspapers stacked represent 72 seconds. If the team took 35 minutes and 22 seconds to run the race, the final total would be 35m/22s minus 1m/12s, giving 34 minutes 10 seconds. There is an extra half point score for each newspaper carried in the race, but not stacked.

The winning team is the one that scores the highest points in the shortest possible time.

51 – The cone hoop-throwing competition

Equipment needed
- 11 road marking cones, numbered as shown (a sympathetic road-works contractor might supply you with these)
- four rubber rings (like those used on the beach).

How to play
This is an ideal inter-schools competition which is popular with young people and it can give PTAs a new source of income from

spectators who pay an entry fee to support their teams. The game can be run on a league basis with a trophy and cash prize for the winning school.

The 11 numbered road marking cones are placed in the positions shown in Figure 24 at a distance of 6 ft from the throwing line.

Each school team submits four members to make a team, and each team is given four rings to throw over the cones. Each person in the team starts with a score of 300 which he must try to reduce to zero by deducting the scores from the cones he has successfully ringed. The first person in each team to reach zero wins the match for the team. There is a total of four matches to a game, with one point only being allowed to the team that wins each match. Hence the team that wins all of its matches will accumulate four points on the league table.

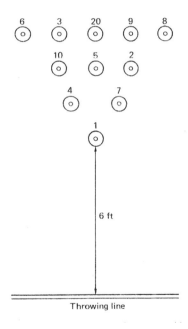

Figure 24 – The cone hoop-throwing competition.

52 – Pub wheelbarrow race

Equipment needed
- four people to each team
- one wheelbarrow for each team
- 16 table-tennis balls (these are shared by all teams competing).

How to play
Persuade four or more pub landlords to agree to cooperate in this venture. Their pubs will be used as venues for the event. The first pub will also be used for the finishing round of the competition.

Teams should assemble in the car park of the pub used for the start of the competition. One player in each team of four is selected as the person to ride in the wheelbarrow *and* play the ball throwing game in each of the pubs. The remaining three members of the team take it in turns to push the wheelbarrow.

At the word 'go' all team members rush into the pub and consume a pint each of their favourite drink. When all four glasses are empty, the ball-throwers queue to play the ball throwing game. It is important for team members to finish their drinks quickly as the game is played in strict order of arrival of the ball-throwers at the game table.

A pint tumbler is placed on a table, 3 ft 6 in. from a starting line, and each thrower is given one table-tennis ball which he must throw into the tumbler. He is allowed five tries. The ball is returned to the player after each miss. If the ball is not in the tumbler after the fifth try, the player must go to the end of the queue and try again.

Once a ball-thrower has succeeded in lodging a ball in the tumbler, that team can push the wheelbarrow to the next pub venue.

At the second pub, team members again consume a round of drinks. This time the throwers are given five chances to throw two table-tennis balls into two separate pint tumblers. Again the throwing distance is 3 ft 6 in. from the throwing line. Throwers go to the end of the queue if they are unsuccessful. If successful the team can continue the race.

At the third pub, players again drink a round but this time three balls must be thrown, one into each of three tumblers. Again the players are given only five throws. If they do not secure all three balls, they must join the end of the queue and try again to get the remaining balls into their tumblers.

At pub number four, the game is repeated but four balls must be placed in tumblers.

Now the teams race back to the pub where they started. They will try to throw five balls into their respective tumblers but here the rules change: the player is given three throws at each tumbler and the total number of balls placed is counted. Two minutes are deducted from the finishing time of the team for each ball that is successfully placed, so if the player throws all five into their respective tumblers, a total of 10 minutes is deducted from his team's time.

The finishing time of all the teams should be recorded, and the team with the shortest finishing time, after deductions in the final round, is declared the winner.

If there are sufficient pubs tied to a brewery in one area, it should be possible to approach the company for sponsorship and prizes for the event. The public should be invited to forecast the finishing order of the teams entering the competition. The nearest to correct answer wins a prize sponsored by the brewery. There can also be a prize for the team that raises the highest amount of sponsorship.

Charge an entry fee of £10 for each team that enters the competition. The entry fee for the competition to forecast the correct finishing order of teams should be 50p per guess.

53 – The ball and cane obstacle relay race

Equipment needed
- one walking cane with a crook at one end for each team member
- one tennis ball for each team
- seven road cones, placed as shown in Figure 25
- a 6 ft long plastic pipe, 3 in in diameter
- a plastic bucket
- two planks, 4 ft x 6 in
- one sheet of hardboard, 8 ft x 4 ft with 4 in diameter hole
- 12 building bricks
- four stools, about 18-24 in high.

Select a route of about 2½ miles. It is essential that the planned route is discussed with the police and local authority who will need to give their support to your use of the public highway. Make sure that the course has a few hills and good sharp bends, because this makes the competition more exciting both for players and spectators.

Recruit your teams from youth clubs, pubs and even from local business organisations. There should be five members to a team, and as many teams as possible from the area where you plan to hold the event.

It is a good idea to start and finish the event in the forecourt of a local pub, if possible on a sunny Sunday morning around 11.30 am. The brewery who own the pub may well sponsor the event in return for the publicity and custom it will attract.

How to play
The race should be divided into five sections, with obstacle courses off the public highway at half-mile intervals.

Contestants are asked to guide the tennis ball along the route with their walking cane. At no time is the ball allowed to be touched by hand. The group should have at least four stewards to supervise the contest and to ensure that all obstacles are negotiated properly, with no rules broken!

The first contestant has to negotiate seven road cones, laid out as shown in Figure 25. The player will then hand over his cane and ball to the next contestant who will run the second half-mile of the race. The second obstacle is a long plastic pipe placed at an angle on three bricks. The contestant has to knock the ball through the pipe and then hand over the ball and cane to the third member of the team.

The third team member must get his ball into a plastic bucket and take it out again, using his cane. At no time must his hands touch the ball.

The fourth obstacle is a 4 ft plank resting on a stool. The player must knock the ball up the plank and down the other side, without allowing it to fall off. If the ball rolls off either side, it is returned to the bottom of the plank so that the player can try again.

The final obstacle is a sheet of hardboard with a hole cut into it. This is placed at an angle, and the player must aim the ball with his crook so that it rolls up the hardboard and through the hole. The ball is then rolled on to the finishing line.

The first team to reach the winning line without cheating is the winner.

This competition is great fun for participants and for spectators. Invite people to take bets on the winning team in order to supplement your income.

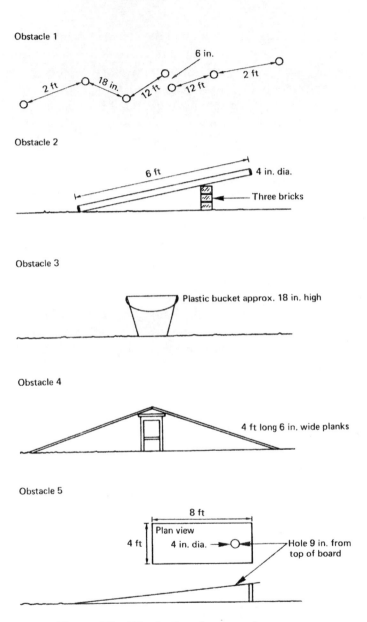

Obstacle 1

Obstacle 2

Obstacle 3

Obstacle 4

Obstacle 5

Figure 25 – The ball and cane relay race

54 – The backwards cycle relay race

Equipment needed
● one cycle for each team.

This event is a very good attraction at an outdoor fete if you have the space. One of the main benefits is that it encourages competing teams to bring along their supporters, who will all pay their entry fees and participate in other competitions at the fete, so boosting your income considerably.

Invite teams of children from schools in the area of your venue. Aim to secure at least 16 teams, with four members to each team. Charge an entry fee of £2 for each team.

How to play
Two cyclists are placed at each end of a 100-yard course. The first team member starts the race by sitting on his handle bars. Pedalling from that position, he cycles with his back towards the finishing line, where the second member of the team is waiting. When he crosses the line, the second member cycles backwards in the same way towards the starting point, where the third member of the team takes over. The fourth member of the team then cycles backwards to finish the race.

Any person who falls from his cycle loses 2 penalty points. Any person who walks more than 3 ft after falling from his bike will also lose 2 points.

The team to complete the race with the least number of penalty points and in the quickest time, wins the race.

The winners of each heat compete in the semi-finals, and the first and second teams in the semi-final go forward to compete in the final. It should be possible to obtain sponsorship for this event from cycle manufacturers, accessory dealers or good sports shops.

A small trophy, with a prize of £100 for the winners and £50 for the 'runners-up', should attract competitors.

Members of the public can be invited to pay 20p to forecast the first, second and third winning teams in the final race. Betting must finish before the start of the race. Offer odds of 3 to 1 against each team, and accept the bets in units of 20p.

Always run this event on grass so that cyclists who fall will not injure themselves.

55 – The bouncing ball racquet relay race

Equipment needed
- one tennis racquet and tennis ball for each team
- each team member to be given a number or colour to distinguish one team from another.

How to play
Ask local clubs, pubs, shops and industry to enter teams of six people in a relay race. Try to persuade at least 12 teams to participate.

The race is over a six-mile circuit. Team members are given a number or colour to distinguish one from another, and the first runs along, bouncing the ball with the racquet. The ball must be kept bouncing all the time until the player reaches the second member of the team, who will continue with the race. The runner hands his next team member the racquet, but the ball should not stop bouncing. If the ball is dropped, the runner must pick it up and start to bounce it again immediately. The first team to reach the finish wins the trophy.

This is a lively and exciting relay race. Members of the team should be asked to find their own sponsors by asking friends, family, and work colleagues and so on, to back their efforts. An entry fee of £10 per team may be charged.

Your group should be able to find a sponsor to offer a worthwhile prize plus a trophy to be competed for on an annual basis for the benefit of your cause. The sponsors can also be asked to supply team members with tee-shirts bearing the sponsor's name on the front and back. Extra funds can be raised by asking people to pay 20p to guess the finishing order of each team in the race, recording the guesses on prepared forms provided for the purpose.

A useful prize for the person guessing the winning team could be a shopping voucher for £50 redeemable at a local shop, with a second voucher for £25 for the person who guesses the second and third winning team, and a cheque for £10 for the person who guesses the correct winning sequence of the remaining teams.

56. The ball and tray relay race

Equipment needed (for each team)
- one plastic tray
- three clear plastic tumblers
- a supply of coloured water
- a 9 in rubber ball
- a 3-pint measure marked in tenths of an inch.

How to play
Persuade as many organisations as possible to enter teams of six members into this race. The course should be between two pubs situated about two miles apart.

The first member of each team is given a plastic tray supporting three clear plastic tumblers filled with coloured water. The tray is held in one hand, and the other is used to bounce a 9 in ball along the road as he runs to meet the next member of the team along the route. The course should be equally divided between all six members of the team. At each checkpoint, the total amount of liquid from the three tumblers is measured, and the tumblers are filled again.

At the end of the competition the winning time is recorded, but 10 seconds are added for each tenth of an inch of liquid that has been lost during the race.

Each team pays £10 to enter the race. Find a sponsor to donate a trophy for the winning team which can be competed for each year. Each member of the team could seek individual sponsors. In this case there could be a second trophy for the team that raises the most money for the charity.

Ask people to guess the time of the winning team, to the nearest second, for a prize. At 25p per guess, this will bring a nice extra income for your cause.

57 – Motor car relay race

Equipment needed
- the same model of car for each team entered
- two ropes for each car.

How to play
Find 17 people to make up each team, comprising a driver and four groups of four people. If you have more than 12 teams competing in the race, then run the event in heats of five or six, (whichever divides equally into your total number of entries).

The length of the course should be 880 yards. A large car park or local running track are both useful venues for this event. If a car park is used, the course should be marked out with road cones.

One member of the team sits in the driving seat and the first four team members have to pull the car with the rope for 220 yards, when they hand over the task to the second four team members. These contestants will pull the car for a further 220 yards, and so on until the fourth team tow the car to the finish. If any of the teams knock over the marking cones, they have to return to the start of their section of the race. If the race is run in heats, the first two teams will go forward to the final.

Each team pays £10 to enter the competition, and the team that raises the most sponsorship from its members wins a prize. Most of the income from this event will come from gambles on the winning team. Odds of 4 to 1 are offered against all teams.

It might be possible to get car manufacturer or dealer to sponsor the event and supply the cars in return for advertising at the event.

Competitions with Teams and People Competing Against Each Other

58 – The keg barrel relay race

Equipment needed (for each team)
- one alloy keg barrel
- nine road cones
- one bottle crate
- two 8 ft wooden planks, at least 10 in. wide.

This is a good project for a main event at an outdoor fete or fair. You will need the cooperation of your local brewery to lend you the alloy keg barrels, and they may also provide you with prizes and a trophy in return for your naming the event after the brewery and for displaying banners at the start and finish advertising the sponsor's name.

How to play
Local pubs and clubs are good outlets for entries, but advertise for teams to enter the race at least ten weeks prior to the event, with four people to a team. If there are sufficient entries, you can run off several heats of four teams. In this case you will need four barrels!

Lay out the course in an oval shape, as shown in Figure 26. This is divided into equal sections, with three different obstacles that must be negotiated with the barrel.

The barrels should be half filled with water as this makes rolling them more difficult for contestants and more fun for spectators to watch.

Each member of the team must try to roll the barrel through each of the three obstacles on the course, if possible without touching the obstacles with the barrel. A helper should be placed at each set of obstacles to ensure that they are properly negotiated and to see that the rules of play are not broken! If a manoeuvre is not made correctly, the player must go back to the start of the obstacle to try again. Each breach of the rules adds 2 minutes to the finishing time.

The game is played in heats of four teams. The first two teams home should progress to the next round until the final three winning teams are known.

The first obstacle is five road cones placed in an S shape. The space between the cones should be the length of the barrel plus 4 in. i.e., about 3 ft.

The second obstacle is a plank placed each side of a bottle crate, and contestants have to wheel the barrel up one plank and down the other side while walking on the planks behind the barrel. If the contestant or his barrel fall from the plank, he must start the obstacle again.

The third obstacle is four cones placed in a square, the space between each being the width of the barrel plus 4 in. Contestants must roll the barrel between cones 1 and 2 and then lead it in a circle around cone 3 and back to the centre of the square. Finally, the barrel is wheeled out through the space between cones 2 and 4.

During each heat you should invite the public to bet on which team will win. Offer odds of 4 to 1 against each team in units of 20p. You can run another competition to forecast the correct order of the first, second and third finalists.

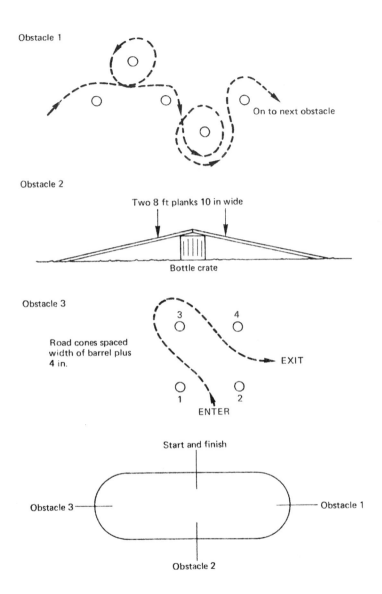

Obstacle 1

On to next obstacle

Obstacle 2

Two 8 ft planks 10 in wide

Bottle crate

Obstacle 3

Road cones spaced
width of barrel plus
4 in.

3 4

EXIT

1 2

ENTER

Start and finish

Obstacle 3

Obstacle 1

Obstacle 2

Figure 26 – The keg relay race

59 – The upside-down walk

Equipment needed
- one tray
- two plastic pint tumblers
- a supply of fresh water
- a ruler or tape measure that shows tenths of an inch.

How to play
Contestants lie on their backs and lift themselves on to their hands and feet to walk with their backs facing the ground for this race. A tray containing two plastic pint tumblers, both filled to the brim with water, is placed on each person's stomach, and at the word 'go' contestants have to race 50 yards towards the finishing line to see who can reach the finish in the shortest time without spilling too much water.

For every tenth of an inch of liquid lost, 1 second is added to the finishing time. The liquid loss can be measured from the top of each glass. Alternatively, use a measuring jug that registers millilitres and pour the remaining water in to take the reading – add 1 second for each 2ml lost. (You will need to know exactly what the full glass holds.)

The winner earns his or her team 20 points; the second gains 15 points; the third 10 points; and the fourth 5 points.

60 – The water squirt

Equipment needed
- one empty washing-up liquid container for each team
- one bucket of water
- one empty bucket.

How to play
The first contestant in each team is given an empty washing-up liquid container and an empty bucket is placed by his side. At the word 'go' he must race 50 yards to a second bucket filled with water. He must

suck as much water as he can into his container, and run back to the starting point to squeeze the liquid into the empty bucket within three minutes. He then gives the container to the next contestant to use. The team that finishes the race with the largest quantity of water in its bucket wins. If there are six members in a team, the game is allowed 18 minutes to finish. At the end of this time, any water in the container is ignored. The winner earns his team 20 points; the second 15 points; the third 10 points; and the fourth 5 points.

61 – The pyramid-carrying obstacle race

Each of the obstacles in this competition can be used as separate fund-raising events, or they can be used in one exciting obstacle course.

Equipment needed (see Figure 27)
- plastic tray with playing blocks

Obstacle 1: The kitchen chair step
- two kitchen chairs

Obstacle 2: The limbo course
- two wooden supports in each of the four following sizes: 1 ft, 18 in, 20in and 24in.
- four lengths of dowelling approx. 4 ft long (to rest between the supports)

Obstacle 3: Climbing through tyres
- three different sizes of car tyre (say, 16 in, 20 in and a lorry tyre).
- three ropes 4 ft long.
- one length of wood to hold the tyres.
- two wooden supports.

Obstacle 4: The see-saw
- one 6 ft plank, 9 in. wide, for each team.
- an oil drum for each team.

Obstacle 5: The brick step
- bricks to make six five-step brick obstacles.

- one large tray for each obstacle.

Obstacle 6: The sewer-pipe crawl
- a sewer pipe, 3 ft long and 2 ft 6 in. in diameter, for each team.

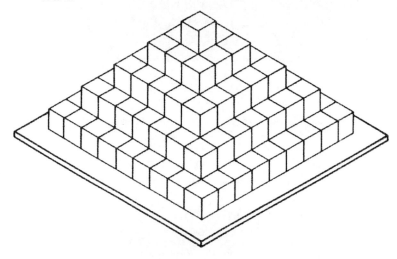

Figure 27a – Pyramid of blocks on tray

How to play

The first member of each team is given a plastic tray with a pyramid of playing blocks. These blocks are five layers high, as shown in Figure 27(a). Each member of the team must carry the tray of blocks over a course 100 yards long, and at the same time negotiate the following six obstacles:

1. The first obstacle is two kitchen chairs placed back to back, with one seat facing towards the team. The team member must run to the first chair, climb onto it, and step across the top onto the seat of the second chair. When both feet rest firmly on the seat of the second chair, he must turn round and step back onto the seat of the first chair, then turn round again and step back onto the ground. Having done this successfully, he must race forward 10 yards to the next obstacle.

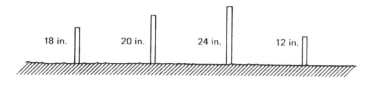

Figure 27b – Cross bar heights

2. Team members have to step over the first limbo cross-bar without knocking it off its two supports (see Figure 27b). They then pass under the second limbo hurdle without putting their free hand on the ground (the 20 in hurdle). At the third hurdle, they step over the obstacle, and at the same time pass the tray from one hand to another underneath the 24 in cross-bar. At the fourth limbo fence, team members jump over the 12 in. hurdle with both feet without allowing the pyramid to fall.

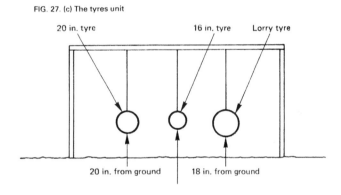

Figure 27c – The tyres unit

3. Team members must pass through each of the tyres (see Figure 27c) without touching them with their feet or hands, while still holding the tray of blocks in one hand.

4. Still carrying the tray of blocks, members of the team run to obstacle four (the see-saw) and walk up the one side of the plank and down the other without jumping (see Figure 27(d)).

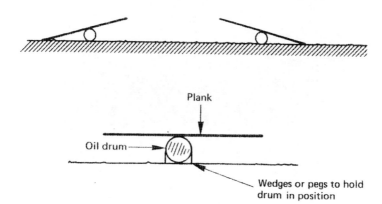

Plank

Oil drum

Wedges or pegs to hold
drum in position

Figure 27d – The see-saw

5. The fifth is a group of five layers of bricks set on a plastic tray. There are six such trays spaced a stepping distance apart. The contestant steps onto the top of the first group and then from one top to another until he completes the course. Every set of bricks he disturbs adds 5 seconds to his time. The six groups can be laid out in a line or in a U shape depending on the space available (see Figure 27e).

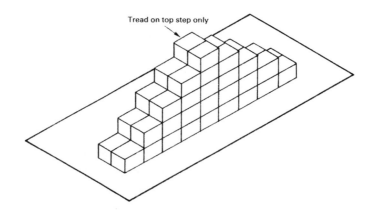

Tread on top step only

Figure 27e – The brick step

6. The team member races to the last obstacle in the race, where he crawls through the pipe, still carrying the tray of bricks which should still be intact in its pyramid shape. As soon as he has negotiated the sewer pipe, he races to the finish.

The second member of the team may start the obstacle race as soon as the first player has replaced any bricks that have fallen from the pyramid and handed the tray over.

Each player loses 5 seconds of time for every block of wood that falls from the pyramid onto the tray. The winner receives 20 points; second 15 points; third 10 points; and fourth 5 points. The team with the largest point score wins the obstacle race.

62 – The oil-drum obstacle race

Equipment needed
- four large empty oil drums
- one plank, 6 in. wide x 6 ft long
- one plank, 6 in. wide x 4 ft long
- one stepladder
- one hook to hang from a cross bar
- three wooden supports
- one measuring container for water
- one goldfish bowl filled with water and suspended on wire
- one chair.

How to play
Contestants are given 3 minutes to complete an obstacle course. During the race each player must carry a goldfish bowl filled with water and suspended on wire, as shown in Figure 28.

1. The contestant climbs onto a chair and then onto an oil drum standing beside it. From here he walks across a 4 ft long plank to a second upturned drum. From the second drum he walks down a 6 ft plank to the ground.

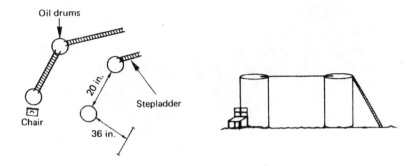

Fish bowl filled with water and suspended on wire

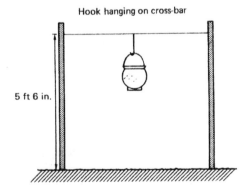

Figure 28 – The oil-drum obstacle race

2. The contestant climbs a stepladder backwards on to the third drum.

3. The contestant now jumps a 20 in. gap to the fourth drum.

4. Once securely on the fourth drum, the contestant leans across a 3 ft gap to hang the fish bowl on the hook suspended from the crossbar on the wooden support.

5. The contestant jumps down from the oil drum and unhooks his fish bowl.

6. Now he must run to the finishing line and pour what is left of the water in his bowl into a measuring container. Two seconds are deducted for each tenth of an inch of water lost.

The person who runs the race in the shortest time wins.

6 – Tennis toss-ball

Equipment needed
- one racquet for each team member
- one tennis ball for each team
- one stopwatch to record the time.

How to play
Find as many teams of eight people as you can, and run the competition in heats of four teams playing at one time. The two teams that finish the game in the quickest time go forward to the next round until the final teams are known.

Team members are lined up either in a big circle or in two straight lines facing one another. The players should be spaced 10 ft apart, and they are not allowed to leave the position they stand in at the start of the game.

The first player in the team hits the ball with his tennis racquet and aims it to land on the racquet of the second member of his team. This member hopes to catch the ball and hold it for two seconds before passing it on to the next player, until it reaches the last member in the team.

If a player drops the ball, he must return it to the previous player to pass to him again. Balls must always be caught by the tennis racquet. Hands may be used only to pick the ball up from the floor. This is a challenging and tricky game to play, and the ball is passed from the first player to the last in the shortest possible time to find the winning teams. The winning team scores 10 points; the second score 8; the third 6; and the fourth 5.

Part 5

INDOOR COMPETITION
EVENINGS

The games that follow can be used for indoor competition evenings. Each can be used as an individual fund-raising event. Alternatively, each player can be asked to play all of the games, and the winner is the person who wins the most points by the end of the evening.

64 – Playing-card relay

Equipment needed
- three packs of playing cards
- three tables
- three chairs
- three stopwatches.

How to play
Players must try each of the card games below, and the winner is the person with the quickest time and the least number of penalty points. This competition makes a good team game, and it can be run off in several heats to find the winning team. No more than three heats should be run at one time.

Game 1
A pack of playing cards is spread out face down, and contestants are given 20 seconds to try to pair together two queens, two kings, two jacks and two aces.

The player loses 5 points for each grouping that he FAILS to achieve in the allotted time.

Game 2
A full pack of cards is placed face down on the table, and the player must try to put together a full suit of cards within 15 seconds from arriving at the table. One point is lost for every card short in the suit at the end of the time.

Game 3
Each card in a set of playing cards is placed face down on a table and contestants have 10 seconds to find the two jokers in the pack. They do this by lifting each card separately, and replacing the cards in the position they were found if the joker is not discovered.

There are 5 points for each joker displayed.

65 – High score dice

Equipment needed
- one plastic cup
- four dice
- one table.

How to play
Each contestant is given three tries to score the highest score with four dice (the total is found by adding together the score of each of the four).

The person with the highest score wins 5 points; the second highest wins 4 points; the third highest wins 3 points; and the fourth highest wins 2 points.

66 – Copper-wire alarm

This unit is cheap and easy to make; it can be used over and over again at indoor events, where you can charge 20p a try.

Equipment needed
- copper-wire alarm unit, as shown in Figure 2
- table
- stopwatch.

How to play
Contestants are given 10 seconds to try to pass the metal ring across the wire frame without touching the wire and sounding the alarm. This game is great fun, but it needs a steady hand. If the metal ring touches the wire, a buzzer will sound and a light will flash. Each time this happens the player loses two points.

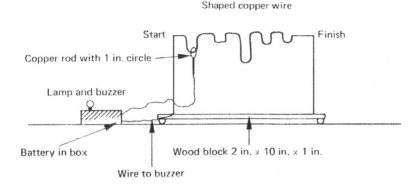

Figure 29 – The copper-wire alarm

67 – Car garaging competition

Equipment needed
- a length of wood sheeting, 24 in. x 10 in
- two strips of wood to raise the board to an angle of about 20° (see Figure 30)
- a length of wood with five 'doorways'
- four 'doorways' 5/8ths of an inch wider than the toy car
- one 'doorway' only 1/2 in. wider than the toy car
- one toy car.

How to play
Players must try to 'garage' the car by allowing it to roll from the starting line down the board in the hope that it will pass through one of the holes at the end of the ramp (see Figure 30).

This game is not as easy as it looks, and it is fun to play. Make sure that the table on which you operate the game is level, or the car will run off the side of the ramp and you could be accused of 'fixing' the game! Charge 20p for each attempt, and offer prizes valued at about £1.50 with a bonus prize for those who successfully negotiate their car through the smallest hole.

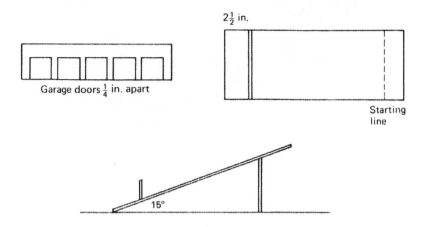

Figure 30 – The car garaging competition

68 – Guess the order of heads up

Equipment needed
- five 2p coins.
- a length of wood, 2 in. wide x 12 in. Long x 1/2 in. thick.
- a length of hardboard, 2 ft x 2 ft.

How to play

Paint six squares, 4 in. x 4 in., on the hardboard, as shown in Figure 31. In each square print a number of heads that can turn up when five coins are spun into the air from the length of wood onto the board. Each square gives a different variation of all possible number of heads that can be thrown from none to five.

Before spinning the coins, the operator asks people to place their bets, at 4 to 1, on which square will show the number of heads they have guessed. Each guess is 20p and these coins are placed on the chosen squares. The operator then spins the 2p coins by flipping the length of wood to throw the coins into the air and onto the board top. To find the winners, the 2p coins are checked to discover how many heads are showing. Those who have put bets on the correct squares are paid 4 to 1 on the money they placed.

This game brings out the gambling instinct in people, and it has proved to be a very big cash taker at both indoor and outdoor events.

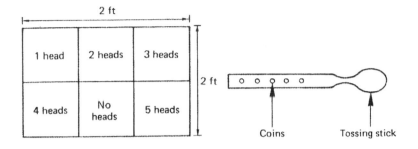

Figure 31 – Guess the order of heads up.

69 – Plasticine game

Equipment needed
- four sticks of Plasticine rolled into 1/2 in balls
- one sheet of glass, 24 in square.
- one strip of chipboard, 48 in x 24 in on which to fix the glass
- wooden frame to support the chipboard.

How to play
Using a felt-tip pen, mark the glass sheet into nine squares, each numbered as in Figure 32. The glass is then fixed to the chipboard and hung onto a wooden support or wall.

157

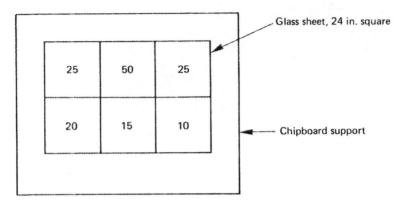

Figure 32 – The Plasticine game

This game is especially suitable for children. For a fee of 10p, a contestant is given four balls of Plasticine which he must throw onto one of the numbered squares on the board from a distance of 4 ft. Only those balls which remain sticking to the glass after the last ball has been thrown can be counted in the score. Players must score over 20 to win a prize. Prizes should be valued at about £1.

70 – Table tennis fling ball

A little more space is needed for this game, but it can be played indoors and it provides an exciting finale to a competition evening. It is also a good fund-raising game at 20p for six balls to throw.

Equipment needed
- 9 ft wooden support (see Figure 33)
- a goldfish bowl
- table tennis balls
- table.

How to play
Six table tennis balls are placed in a container on the table in front of

158

the player. He or she has to throw each ball a distance of 6 ft from the stand, and try to land it in the goldfish bowl hanging from its wooden support.

Two points are given for each ball that lands in the bowl. Players must score 10 points to win a prize valued at £2. An 8-point score wins a £1 prize.

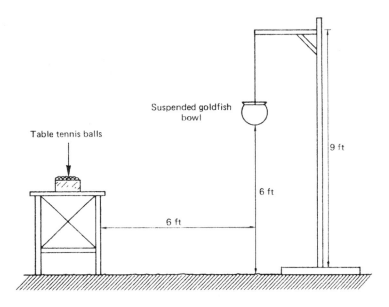

Figure 33 – Table tennis fling ball

Part 6

SOME UNUSUAL MONEY-SPINNERS TO ATTRACT THE CROWDS

71 – Advance ticket count competition

This competition is designed to persuade people to attend your fund-raising event even if the weather is bad and attendances would normally be poor!

First you find a sponsor who will donate an attractive prize to your cause. A holiday or a prize of similar value would be ideal. Now have printed as many advance tickets as you can hope to sell in the weeks prior to your event. They must all be numbered in consecutive order. The holders of these pre-paid entry tickets are entitled to a free entry into a ticket count com- petition on the day.

How to play

Ticket holders are asked to select a numbered cloakroom ticket from a drum. They then add the number on their entry ticket to the number on their cloakroom ticket, and this total number is given to the organiser who will write the figure down on a sheet of lined paper, together with the ticket holder's name and address. (For example, if someone has bought ticket number 459 and then picks cloakroom ticket number 10, the total of 469 is recorded).

To save people queuing to have their draw number recorded, contestants can write their score, together with their name and address, on their entry form, and place it in a special container. One of the organisers can then fill in the details on prepared charts at leisure.

Before the end of the fete, a member of the public is invited to draw one number from a drum, and this total score wins the prize. This game is more exciting than a straightforward ticket draw and introduces additional suspense because it requires the ticket holder to do something positive before he can win the prize. Another advantage of this competition is that it does not come under the control of the Gaming and Lotteries Acts because a degree of skill and action is required by contestants.

To ensure quick location of the winner, it is best to record the ticket totals as closely as possible in numerical order. If the first number drawn fails to find a winner, then another number is drawn and so on until one is found. To encourage sponsors, offer to have their names printed on the entry forms.

72 – Find the cosmetics competition

This competition is very much for the benefit of women, and it is very popular with all who are interested in cosmetics and beauty care.

The competition should be organised over as wide an area as possible, with the sponsorship and support of a cosmetics manufacturer and the cooperation of several retail outlets that stock the company's products. The manufacturer, or competition organiser, must arrange for retail outlets to have a special window display of all the various products that are manufactured by the sponsor. These displays should be on view for all to see from a specified date and for the duration of the competition.

Ask your sponsor to have the entry forms printed because you are offering good publicity for his products. The sponsor's name can be printed on the forms to advertise the firm, and the names of the products can be hidden in a rectangle of letters shown on the entry form (see Figure 34).

How to play

Contestants buy entry forms for 25p and go to any of the shops that are showing the window display. They then write down the name of each product on show on the left-hand side of the form.

Now contestants search the rectangle of letters carefully to find the names of all the products that they have listed. Two will have been deliberately omitted to make the game more of a challenge. The names may be hidden diagonally, up and down, and back to front. When a name is found, the contestant circles it with a pen.

When all products are circled, contestants should describe in not more than 35 words how they can use one of the products to obtain its full benefit.

The winning entry will be an all correct marking of products in the rectangle, a correct list of products listed on the entry form, and the most pleasing description of how one of the products can be used to benefit the user!

Entry forms should be placed in boxes provided inside the shops

Here is a chance to win a £250 voucher for the purchase of cosmetics by .... There are four prize vouchers to be won, and they can be used in any of the following stores taking part in the competition: ....

HOW TO ENTER

After you have purchased an entry form, you should take it to any of the stores listed above, and write down the name of all .... products shown in the window display, on the left-hand side of this form.

Now try to locate these products amongst the rectangle of letters on the right side of this form. Ring them with a pen, and in not more than 35 words write down how you would use your favourite product to its best advantage.

All entries that have all the items correctly recorded and outlined in the rectangle will have their written entry judged by a panel of experts.

RULES AND CONDITIONS OF ENTRY

1. Entries will be accepted only on an official entry form.

2. The entry form must be in the possession of the organisers by the closing date.

3. The judges' decision is final and binding on all contestants and no correspondence will be entered into concerning the competition.

4. The 25p entry fee is a contribution to the appeal fund for ....

5. You may send in as many entries as you wish so long as they are on a proper entry form.

Continued overleaf

List products on show in the special window displays here:

H	E	I	L	D	R	E	D	W	O	P	M	U	C	L	A	T	A	E	O	P	L	O	C
A	A	B	O	C	L	I	P	S	T	I	C	K	O	A	D	H	J	Y	P	A	O	S	O
N	S	A	E	M	I	X	I	N	S	P	G	I	N	I	C	F	K	E	N	O	L	T	A
D	T	E	G	U	O	R	A	A	A	E	W	B	A	T	H	O	I	L	M	F	P	L	R
C	R	A	M	M	E	I	S	N	O	X	A	U	C	F	O	T	Y	I	U	O	O	A	N
R	I	C	L	E	A	N	S	I	N	G	L	O	T	I	O	N	E	N	I	U	Z	S	O
E	N	M	O	N	A	T	B	T	R	V	G	I	O	S	K	J	L	E	M	N	O	H	S
A	G	E	N	Z	I	X	V	S	U	M	S	O	B	A	Z	E	K	R	O	D	G	T	E
M	E	K	A	C	N	D	O	A	Z	R	F	K	N	O	L	P	R	V	H	A	J	A	A
H	N	O	K	E	E	N	R	B	U	W	I	V	M	A	D	R	H	M	O	T	O	B	R
S	T	A	L	C	Y	A	V	W	I	J	C	S	T	D	G	Y	R	I	U	I	L	G	E
I	N	V	I	E	C	C	Z	E	B	Y	B	P	E	N	C	I	L	J	N	O	N	O	D
N	X	O	X	S	T	O	W	B	I	V	Z	S	V	R	S	F	O	O	S	N	X	Z	W
R	A	E	A	H	E	L	B	K	F	G	O	J	Z	X	N	B	D	F	T	T	V	A	O
A	I	M	D	A	A	O	A	R	E	N	H	S	E	R	F	N	I	K	S	I	L	G	P
V	E	U	L	D	E	G	C	O	R	Z	X	O	U	V	W	E	N	K	T	N	O	D	M
L	A	F	E	O	K	N	F	L	U	I	D	M	A	K	E	U	P	D	M	G	L	N	A
I	N	R	O	W	R	E	D	W	O	P	T	N	E	C	U	L	S	N	A	R	T	C	E
A	X	E	D	E	O	R	M	A	N	E	X	O	T	V	W	B	L	K	M	O	P	E	R
N	O	P	E	K	O	W	I	X	M	E	Y	E	C	R	E	A	M	O	S	A	K	W	C

Name

Address

Telephone

In more more than 35 words, tell us the best possible way to use your favourite .... Product.

Figure 34 – Sample entry form for the cosmetics competition.

taking part in the competition, or they may be returned by post to the secretary, whose name and address will appear on the entry form. The competition should run from a period of four weeks to a maximum of 15.

Judges should be drawn from people engaged in the field of cosmetics and beauty care who are qualified to judge the written appraisal of a beauty product. Offer good prizes that will have a strong appeal, valued at say £250 for each of four winning entries. An added attraction could be a visit to see the cosmetics being made at the manufacturer's premises. A combined prize could be a holiday weekend and supply of the company's products, or a cosmetic gift voucher redeemable at any of the shops taking part in the competition.

From the point of view of the manufacturer, this competition is an advertising gimmick they cannot ignore because, for a very low cost, they can promote and advertise their products in a quite unique way.

Shopkeepers will be happy to participate in a scheme like this because it attracts people to look in their shop windows, where they may see other items on display that they might like to buy. In fact, shopkeepers will often pay a contribution towards the cost of printing forms and posters, or they may give a cash donation in return for the publicity they will receive.

73 – I spy the odd man out

For this competition, you need the cooperation of at least 25 retail shops and stores in your area. One unusual item is placed in each shop window display, positioned carefully so that contestants have to study the entire display to find the 'odd man out'. (This should be an item that is not normally for sale in the shop.)

Provide an entry form similar to the one illustrated in Figure 35. On this form, 30 items are listed, numbered 1-30. Five of the items, although written on the list, will not be hidden in the windows. This provides an extra challenge for contestants. (Make sure that the five missing items are not being shown unwittingly as part of the normal display!)

The entry form lists the names and addresses of all shops and stores taking part in the competition. Each firm is given a letter of the alphabet to distinguish them and help contestants:

When a contestant locates a hidden item, the appropriate letter of the alphabet is written in the column provided on the entry form to indicate the shop or store where it was found.

All the shops and stores taking part in this competition should be asked to contribute £15 in return for the promotional benefits they are likely to receive from the publicity and from people looking at their window displays. A shopping voucher or a hamper worth £100 would be a suitable prize for the winner, with prizes of a lesser value for second and third runners-up.

ERDINGTON AND DISTRICT COMMUNITY GROUP
'I SPY THE ODD MAN OUT' COMPETITION
WIN A £50 SHOPPING VOUCHER

Below you will find a list of 30 items. 25 of which will be placed in the window displays of 25 shops in Erdington and District. The name and address of each shop is printed on the left-hand side of this form.

Visit all the shops listed below, and try to locate one of the 30 items on this list which is found in each window display. Five of the items listed are surplus and cannot be found in any of the displays.

When you have found an item, write down alongside it the letter allocated to the shop (see below).

When you have located all the items, send your entry form to ....
....
or deposit it in the box provided at any of the following shops
....
The first all correct entry form drawn from a drum at High Street Shopping Centre on .... at 3 pm will be declared the winner.

Items hidden	Write the letter given to the shop where item was found	Shops and stores participating	
Oxo cube	D	A	Marshall's D.I.Y. Store
Postage stamp	...	B	Dixon's Wool Shop
Small glass marble	...	C	Herron Butchers
£1 coin	...	D	Eileen's Florist
Button	...	E	etc.....
etc.			

Name ....
Address ....
.... Postcode ....
Entry fee 25p

Figure 35 – Sample entry form for the 'odd man out' competition.

74 – Hospital radio bingo

Equipment needed
- 99 table tennis balls, numbered 1 to 99
- bag to hold the table tennis balls
- bingo cards.

How to play

This game can be played at agreed times on a hospital radio station. The disc jockey picks table tennis balls at random from a cloth bag, and calls out the number printed on the ball. (The used balls are then placed in a second bag so that numbers can be checked if necessary.)

Patients pay 25p for each game. An assistant on each ward sells the bingo cards, and phones in to the radio station as soon as a patient has filled in a line of five numbers on a card. The numbers should be called out slowly to give patients time to tell the caller that a line has been won and for this message to be relayed to the disc jockey.

Patients have a lot of time to spare in hospital, and they welcome this form of entertainment. The hospital league of friends can therefore benefit from a regular income from this type of competition.

Small prizes or vouchers may be donated by local traders, with a top value of about £5 for a full house and £3 for each line completed first. If you have a selection of prizes valued at £5, patients may either accept the lower-value gift for one line, or wait for a bigger prize if they get the full house.

75 – Hospital pontoon: score 21 to win

I first introduced this game to a League of Hospital Friends in 1968 and it has proved to be a popular money-spinner and a regular source of income for this fund-raising group ever since. Patients say they enjoy the excitement of the game and it breaks the monotony of a hospital stay.

Equipment needed
- pontoon score cards (see Figure 36)
- pack of playing cards
- a sweet jar painted a bright colour so that the contents cannot be seen.

How to play
All the patients in the hospital wards are invited to take part in this game. For a fee of 25p they are given a pontoon score card and a chance to draw three cards from the sweet jar to try to score 21. Alternatively, patients can draw one card only from the jar, and this score is recorded on the pontoon card which they keep in their possession. The draw is then repeated each day until a player scores 21. If no one has scored 21 by each Friday, then the score nearest to 21 wins the prize. Ace scores 1 or 11; jack, queen and king score 10. Prizes should be goods or vouchers donated from local pubs, shops and business organisations.

PONTOON SCORE CARD No 7		
Please retain this card during the game so that your score can be checked		
1st card	2nd card	3rd card
Name _____ Total _____		

Figure 36 – Hospital pontoon score card

76 – Park the caravan

Equipment needed
- one two-berth caravan
- one stopwatch
- 40 road cones
- 10 bamboo canes
- 10 wooden blocks, approx. 4 in x 4 in x 3 in to hold the canes
- 6 lengths of timber, 4 in x 4 in square and 7 ft 6 in Long
- a clear starting line and finishing line
- a length of 1 in dowel to fit across entrance supports of one enclosure.

How to erect obstacles (see Figure 37)

Obstacle 1
- Place the road cones in position, as illustrated. Arrow signs should mark the route. The space between all cones should be 18 in wider than the caravan.

Obstacle 2
- The bamboo cane course should be constructed as shown, with arrows to show the route. Each cane should be spaced 24 in. wider than the caravan.

Obstacles 3 and 4
- These are placed side by side and constructed with the six lengths of timber, placed as shown in the diagram, so that the supports are 6 in. wider than the caravan and 9 in Longer than its length. A length of dowel is placed across the supports of the entrance of the second enclosure. This should be suspended 2 in higher than the maximum height of the caravan.

How to play
Teams of three people are invited to push the caravan by hand from its starting point and round the obstacle course. First the caravan is manoeuvred around the cones. The cones must not be touched, moved or knocked over. If they are touched, 30 seconds are added to the finishing time.

171

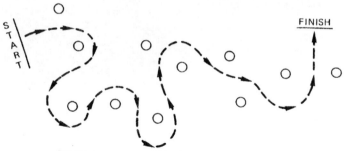

Space between cones width of caravan + 18 in.

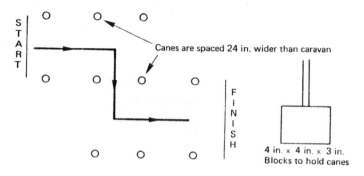

Canes are spaced 24 in. wider than caravan

4 in. x 4 in. x 3 in.
Blocks to hold canes

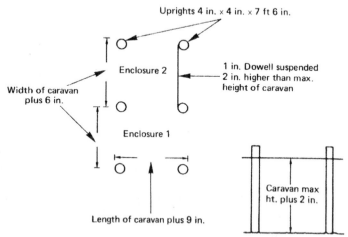

Uprights 4 in. x 4 in. x 7 ft 6 in.

Enclosure 2

1 in. Dowell suspended
2 in. higher than max.
height of caravan

Width of caravan
plus 6 in.

Enclosure 1

Length of caravan plus 9 in.

Caravan max
ht. plus 2 in.

Figure 37 – The caravan course

The caravan is then pushed carefully through the maze of cones without touching any of them; 30 seconds are added to the finishing time for every cone touched by a person or the caravan.

The caravan is then manoeuvred into the first enclosure. Again 30 seconds is added to the time if the wooden supports are touched. Finally, the most difficult manoeuvre of all is to pull the caravan out of the first enclosure and into the second without touching the dowelling or making it fall; 30 seconds is added to the finishing time for any movement of the wooden supports or dowelling.

The time of each team is checked with a stopwatch from start to finish. The team with the shortest time and the least number of faults wins the prize.

Teams pay a fee of £2 to enter the race and members of the public are invited to pay 15p to guess the winning team and win a prize.

A maximum of 15 teams is recommended for this event if it is used at a fete. This gives people time both to watch the race and to try their luck on other stalls. Try to get teams from local pubs and clubs. These are usually good sources for entries into this competition.

The game should be insured against injury to players or spectators. Try to persuade an insurance firm or an insurance broker to sponsor the event in return for suitable advertising.

The caravan may be borrowed from a caravan manufacturer or dealer in return for advertising on and around the caravan. To encourage a good sponsor, the event could be named after the person or firm backing the event.

77 – The pillar-box contest

Equipment needed
- the loan of a selected pillar-box in your area
- a large number of envelopes of varying sizes and shapes
- sheets of paper to be put into each envelope.

How to play
Contestants pay 20p to guess how many envelopes can be posted in a

specific letter box at any one time. Guesses are recorded on a prepared chart, with the name and address of each contestant, and the person who guesses nearest to the correct number of envelopes wins the prize. A postman will probably allow your group to have a trial run prior to the event in order to determine approximately how many envelopes will be needed. It is not easy to guess the correct number because of the wide variety in size and shapes used, but you must ensure that you are not short of envelopes on the day.

The competition must be done in public. You will need the attendance of a postman to remove any mail already in the box before the event begins, and to open the box so that you can remove all the envelopes at the finish.

(More envelopes can be put into the pillar box if they are tied with rubber bands!)

78 – Bottle out to sea

This is an exciting competition, and the aim is to find whose bottle will travel the furthest out to sea.

How to play

Invite people to buy a ticket, similar to the one illustrated in Figure 38, for a fee of 25p. Contestants fill in the details on the ticket. The form will be returned to your group inside a clean bottle with a tightly fitting screw top to ensure that the ticket is not lost or destroyed (sauce bottles are particularly suitable).

On a specified date, the competition organisers arrange for the bottles to be taken several miles out to sea. All the bottles will then be released into the water at one spot. The owners of fishing boats and ferries are only too pleased to use their boats to take members of the public to watch the spectacle of the bottles being launched into the water. The competition gives them good business and publicity.

Bottles travel far and wide out to sea, and the winner is the person whose message is returned to your group from the furthest distance away within a period of say, 90 days of launching the bottles.

To encourage people to return the tickets from abroad, offer a prize of £25, paid in the currency of the finder, for the ticket that has travelled further than any other in the competition. (Details are printed on the entry form.)

If you get sponsorship from a sauce manufacturer, insist that all bottles used in the competition are the standard size and shape of their brand. With the good promotion and publicity this offers the manufacturer, you should be able to obtain a substantial prize for the owners of the three bottles that have travelled the furthest distance.

(front of form)

(back of form)

The Sauce Bottle out to Sea
Competitor's No ....
Date bottle released ....
This competition is operated by the organisers under the rules laid down. All competitors are bound by the rules.
(Name of organising body)
The Secretary.
12 Anywhere Place,
Anywhere,
United Kingdom

To the finder of this card
This bottle was released into the Atlantic Ocean from a ferry as a project to raise funds for charity.
If you find the bottle before (closing date) please return the form in it to the address shown overleaf. If it has travelled further than any other. you will be sent a prize of £25. payable in the currency of your country.
Thank you for your support
Name of finder ....
Address ....
....
....
Date found ....
Location of bottle found ....
....

Figure 38 – Sample entry form

79 – Bottle down the river

This race is great fun for any group that is fortunate enough to have a fast-flowing river in their area.

Contestants provide their own wine or spirit bottle. The type of bottle will depend on which firm will sponsor the competition. The manufacturer's label is left intact, but people can decorate their bottles in any way they wish to distinguish them from the rest of the bottles.

How to play

For 50p, each contestant is given an entry card on which they print their name, address and phone number. Each card is then placed inside a bottle tightly sealed with a cork or screw-top lid.

On the day of the race, a large strip of wood is held in place in the centre of the river by ropes secured on each bank. This will hold all the bottles in place until you are ready for the 'off'. The bottles are then allowed to float down the river for, say, two miles, where the winning bottle will be caught in a fisherman's net by someone in a wet suit. The bottle is then opened to find the winning ticket.

Further down the river, all the remaining bottles should be caught by a barrier similar to the starter plank. Arrangements must also be made for the disposal of the bottles at the end of the day.

Choose a section of the river that has plenty of bends and curves for the bottles to negotiate and where members of the public will be allowed to come close to watch. Water board officials will give you the advice you need, including details about currents and fast-flowing areas of water.

80 – Sand designing competition

If your group is near a coastal area where there is a sandy beach, you can organise this very popular game during the holiday season. It is fun for adults as well as for children, and it can be a very profitable fund-raising venture.

One day a week, invite people to draw pictures in the sand to depict a theme given by the organisers. Each picture should take up an area of sand of about 8 ft x 4 ft. Participants should be allowed to bring their own 'props' in the form of shells, stones or paper decorations, and they bring their own brushes, spades and sticks to make their picture.

For a fee of 50p, each contestant is given an entry card with a number. This he or she keeps on display to facilitate the judging. Members of the public are invited to pay 20p to guess the order of the first four winners. They place their names and guesses (numbered 1 to 4) on a card and hand it to the organiser. The person who guesses nearest to the correct winning order of entries wins the prize. Should there be more than one winner, the winning entries are placed in a box and shuffled, and a member of the public is then invited to select the winning ticket.

Events like this always attract a crowd of people. When the competition is run regularly, it becomes quite competitive because people enjoy thinking of new ideas, more original than other competitors, and they are quite happy to bring their own props to adorn their handiwork. (The props must be dismantled by each contestant at the end of the competition.)

There are manufacturers who are often willing to sponsor this event with prizes. If the theme of the drawings is connected with the sponsor's products, it provides a popular means of advertising the firm. For example, the local baker might suggest the theme of 'The bread of life' as their theme for a competition.

Drawings must be completed within an hour of the start of the competition, and judging must be by an impartial person who is knowledgeable about art.

81 – Buy a brick (and win a chance to have a building named after you)

This fund-raising competition is ideal for a group that is set to raise money for a new building or extension.

Equipment needed
- printed cardboard ticket 'bricks' 2½ in x 1 in, with the words PRIZE, LUCKY DRAW CONTESTANT, or TRY AGAIN printed on the face. (This wording is concealed by a peel-off label or scratch-patch which is removed by the person buying the ticket. You will probably need to use the services of a professional security printer with experience of this type of work, to make the tickets appealing and 'official' looking.)

How to play
The card ticket 'bricks' are sold for 50p each. Contestants buy a card in the hope of taking part in the draw or winning a prize. If they win the draw they have the privilege of naming the building.

The draw should take place at the finale of another fundraising attraction, like a country music dance. There is no limit on the number of tickets that one person can buy, but the name drawn from the drum will be the person to name the new extension or building.

The attraction of this competition is that people like the idea of naming a building or extension after themselves or a loved one, and the winner will enjoy the excitement of eventually unveiling the plaque that tells the world how the building was named.

If the PRIZE card is drawn, the prize should be available for collection on the closing date of the competition after the main winner of the competition has been drawn.

Start selling tickets well in advance of the event, and encourage local shops and business people to enter the competition. It should attract industrial and commercial entries because big business names have a unique form of publicity if they win the competition.

82 – Buy a flag and chance a prize

Equipment needed
- entry form tickets
- sticky tags to be worn on clothing (which can be printed with your sponsor's advertisement).

How to play
This event should be advertised well in advance. People pay 20p to wear a flag, and have an opportunity of winning a prize if they are stopped by a helper of the fund-raising group.

The helpers walk amongst the crowds and ask selected ticket-wearers two questions about the sponsor's product. If the questions are answered correctly, the person has his or her name and address written on a card and this is put into a box ready for a public draw later that day.

This competition offers good publicity for a sponsor, and you should be able to get attractive prizes for the first three winners. You may be able to persuade your local television or radio station or local newspaper to sponsor this event. This would help to publicise your cause cheaply and well. Your sponsors will advise about the questions to ask in the competition.

83 – Walk-about competition

Equipment needed
- a large number of small strips of card, 2 in. x 1/2 in., printed with a selection of first names of men and women (at least three cards showing each name is suggested)
- a bag to hold the cards
- prepared charts, held in place on a clipboard
- a basket to hold a selection of small prizes.

How to play
Ask people to choose a name and write this down on a prepared chart.

They now pay 10p to draw a card from the bag. If the name on the card drawn is the same as the name written on the ruled sheet, the contestant can choose a prize from the basket.

The prizes can be vouchers or tokens worth up to £2 or so which are redeemable at local shops. Alternatively, bigger prizes can be offered, to be on show and secretly numbered from 1 to 50. If a player selects the same name that he gave to the helper, he can choose a number. The list of numbers and prizes is written out of sight on the underside of the clipboard, and at a glance the helper can tell the contestant the prize he has won.

The public enjoy this game, and so do the helpers. If your prizes are donated, you can earn quite a lot of money for your cause at very little expense.

If you want helpers to walk around shopping precincts, you will need to gain permission from the owners or from the local authority to ensure that you are not breaking any by-laws.

Name of contestant	Name guessed	Prizes			
		No	Prize	No	Prize
		1	Bottle wine		
		2	Box chocs		
		3	Petrol		
		4	etc.		
		5			
		6			
		7			

Figure 39 – Walk-about competition entry form

84 – Some useful ideas for prizes

Vouchers for goods at any of the following stores make good prizes and are often available if you visit the store management concerned, with a professional approach and a sound proposal:

- garages (for petrol)
- supermarkets, shops and stores
- furniture companies
- electrical or radio shops
- DIY store
- garden centres
- jewellers
- railway or bus company (for free travel)
- breweries (to entitle the holder to drink at any of their tied houses)
- hairdressers or beauty salons.

Vouchers give a degree of publicity to sponsors, and as they can sell their goods at wholesale prices it costs less than donating money. Consider also the following possibilities:

- a holiday for two in London
- restaurant meals
- free theatre tickets
- free driving lessons
- a chance to read the news on a local radio station
- a continental tour
- a gallon of whisky
- a week on a health farm
- an adventure weekend
- a course of instruction in water ski-ing or other sport
- a pony-trekking weekend

In each of the above, the type of sponsor to approach will be obvious.